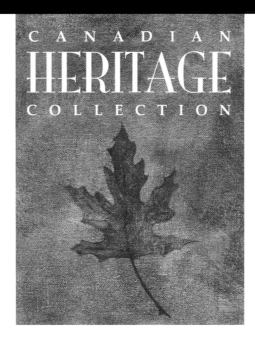

CANADIAN
HERITAGE
COLLECTION

LABOUR AND SOCIAL REFORM

Miriam Bardswich & Sandra Fryer

Series Editor
Don Kendal

Ru'bicon

To Jim for his love and support. Miriam

To Stephen, Aaron and the Beardmores for all their love, patience and support. Sandy

I would like to acknowledge the assistance of Inessa Petersen, Public Programs Coordinator at The Workers Arts and Heritage Centre in Hamilton, Ontario. And, I wish to especially thank Elizabeth Bardswich, Vi Capetelli and "Nellie" for their personal stories. They make history "come alive." –Miriam

I would like to acknowledge the generous assistance of Olivia Rovinescu, Director, Concordia Centre for Teaching and Learning Services. –Sandra

Rubicon Publishing gratefully acknowledges the following for "going above and beyond" in helping us to create this book: Canada Post Corporation, Canadian Press, City of Toronto Archives, and York University.

Rubicon © 2002 Rubicon Education Inc.

Editorial Coordinator: Martine Quibell
Design/Production: Jennifer Drew

National Library of Canada Cataloguing in Publication

Bardswich, Miriam
        Labour and social reform / Miriam Bardswich, Sandra Fryer.

(Canadian heritage collection)
Includes bibliographical references and index.
ISBN 0-921156-86-3

        1. Labor movement—Canada—History—20th century—Sources.
2. Canada—Social conditions—20th century—Sources. 3. Canada—Social policy.
I. Fryer, Sandra II. Title. III. Series: Canadian heritage collection (Oakville, Ont.)

HD8106.5.B37 2002   331.8'0971'0904   C2002-904312-3

Printed in Canada

COVER ART:
Artist: Shannon Olliffe, courtesy of the Mayworks
Festival of Working People and the Arts, www.mayworks.ca

Table of Contents

INTRODUCTION

IMAGINE A CANADA without: "the weekend," eight-hour workdays, child labour laws, minimum wage, labour unions, unemployment insurance, old age pensions, free public education, universal suffrage, public sewer systems, public hospitals, health care, and child and animal protection agencies. Or a Canada in which you face overt racial, gender, and sexual discrimination, or don't have the freedom to practise your religious beliefs. Or a Canada without the Charter of Rights and Freedoms. This was the Canada before labour and social reformers took up the challenge of bringing about change.

In 1872, when the country was only five years old and consisted of six provinces and vast stretches of "empty" land known as Districts, Canada was coping with cultural, social, political, and economic changes brought on by the Industrial Revolution. Expansion of transportation networks was the priority as John A. Macdonald's government struggled to implement the National Policy: to build the Canadian railway from East to West, to protect budding Canadian industries with tariffs, and to fill the land with immigrants. The result was a country with new, urban centres that attracted entrepreneurs and job seekers to meet the labour requirements of industrial growth. In the traditional rural setting, farmers, loggers, miners, fishers, and First Nations people found their lives being transformed by the incursions of new types of machinery, by changing political boundaries, and eventually by the influx of immigrants.

As Canada tried to deal with these realities, there were members of the "new society" who found themselves marginalized by the very society that promised "new beginnings and a better life." Canada actively recruited labour from other countries to fill its growing needs. Despite numerous opportunities, labourers soon found themselves in conflict with their employers and the new industrial standards. Skilled Canadian workers tried to preserve their crafts, working conditions, and wages by forming trade unions such as the United Brotherhood of Carpenters and Jointers of Halifax and the Coopers International Union.

A bitter strike in 1872 by members of the Toronto Typographical Society demanding a 54-hour work week was declared illegal and 24 leaders were jailed. This led to the passing of Canada's first law specifically recognizing the rights of workers to form unions and bargain collectively for better wages, shorter hours of work, and safer working conditions. As a result, "trade unions" were able to give the experienced craftsmen more control over wages and the methods of wage payment; the hours, scheduling, and assignment of work; recruitment, hiring, layoff, and transfer of workers; training and promotion of personnel; the choice and maintenance of equipment; and other related conditions of work such as the quantity and quality of the product.

The craftsmen closely guarded admission to their ranks, but the introduction of labour- and time-saving machinery ultimately limited the amount of control the craft unions enjoyed. Eventually, the segregation of craft workers from the general labour force proved divisive as most of the "new" labour force consisted of semi-skilled or unskilled men, women, and children who had little control of anything in their working lives.

In an age where there were few government services, working conditions for most were terrible. Attempts by industry owners to keep production costs low and profits high meant that wages were low and the workday long and unsafe. Twelve-hour shifts were common. For women, the pay was even lower, the tasks were even more repetitive and menial, and they had to look after their homes and children as well. Neither the government nor the factory owners were concerned about the female work environment, a point made clear during the Royal Commission on Capital and Labour, an investigation into the relationship between employer and employee. This, combined with a lack of a government social safety net (e.g. unemployment insurance, minimum wage, workers' compensation, daycare) and low wages, resulted in many working class families having to put their children to work in order to make ends meet.

Children were very poorly paid and even beaten in their places of work, in factories, shops, homes of their neighbours, their own homes, and on the street. Working class children didn't attend school regularly and were denied opportunities that better skills and knowledge would have given them — opportunities that children of middle and upper class families took for granted.

As wage earners, many immigrants faced poor work conditions and exclusion because of the colour of their skin or their country of origin. Many Anglo-Canadians held the racist belief that "real" Canadians faced "dangers…posed by [immigrants] who could not be assimilated…dangers of dilution and contamination of national blood, national grit, national government, national ideas.…" (Agnes C. Laut, *The Canadian Commonwealth*, 1915)

Those of "non-desirable" origins faced open and systemic discrimination and prejudice, in terms of the type of jobs to which they were given access, when they worked (for example, as strike-breakers during strikes), working conditions, and wages. In British Columbia, unions connected with the Vancouver Trades and Labour Council successfully petitioned the government to stem the flow of "cheap" (i.e. Chinese, Japanese, and Sikh) labour. The Laurier government, in response to the concerns of capital, passed laws such as the Alien Labour Act, designed to prevent foreigners from coming into Canada as contract labour. Mine owners were accused of undermining wages when Italians came to Slocan, B.C. This action represented only one instance where the bosses exploited the fears of the wage earners and used Asians or other workers of "different" ethnic origin as "scabs" (strike-breakers) during job actions. It was only when bigger, more industrial, and more radical unions like the Industrial Workers of the World (IWW) and the Knights of Labour began promoting unionization and organization of the entire working class, rather than protection of specialized trades and its members, that there was more solidarity among all working men and women. The labour movement's struggles highlighted the need for reform by government, capital, and labour.

Reform was needed in other areas of society as well. By the late 1890s, immigration had created a shift in the country's demographics. First Nations people were confined to reserves as the federal government bought their land for settlement by the new immigrants. It was felt that Anglo-Saxon efforts and moral virtues had led to the growth of Canada; and that when left to their own devices, First Nations people were incapable of participating in the political, social, and economic life of Canada. Their lifestyle was rapidly transformed to one involving settlement on reserves, control by government agents, and assimilation in residential schools and by churches. Native groups struggled to cope with the effects of racism, poverty, and the loss of their culture.

Changing provincial boundaries and the growth of cities, new and old, led many rural dwellers, unable to survive on the land, to the cities to seek their fortunes. In addition, large numbers of immigrants flooding into the larger cities meant that there were more job seekers than jobs. Those job seekers began looking West — and Westerners immediately viewed them as a threat to their livelihood. Many members of the working class, the poor, and the newly-arrived immigrants were hampered by poor education, lack of skills, and little or no knowledge of English. They found themselves working for low wages and living in squalid, crowded accommodations, with no safe places for children to play and few, if any, sanitation services. Outbreaks of disease were common and mortality rates, especially among children, were high. There was a desperate need for reform.

Many members of the middle and upper classes took it upon themselves to look after the needs of the poor and other marginalized groups in Canadian society. Not only was it a part of the Social Gospel movement, and a chance to "do good," in the case of children, it gave the middle class reformers a chance to "Canadianize" the poor youth, young immigrants, and First Nations groups. Under their leadership emerged organizations like Public Library Boards, Public Health Boards, Children's Hospitals, Women's Institutes, YMCA and YWCA, and Children's Aid and Humane Societies. Since many of these organizations were founded and chaired by women, and relied on women workers and volunteers, they also represented the beginnings of a women's movement in Canada that would soon turn its attention to organizing to win the right to vote.

Throughout the 20th century, and indeed into the 21st century, Canadian reformers have continued to make the public aware of the need for change. Major events like the Great Depression and the two World Wars have also helped transform Canada. The early reformers were willing to challenge traditional society and agitate for changes that would lead to better working conditions, more equitable standards of living, and policies of inclusion rather than exclusion — changes that many in Canadian society enjoy today. These reformers also demonstrated that social change takes time, sometimes decades, or even a full century. First Nations groups, the governments of Canada, and the courts are currently determining compensation packages for past abuses. The Japanese Canadian community received a token compensation as settlement for their internment during World War II. The descendants of Chinese who were required to pay the Head Tax in order to immigrate have also asked for compensation.

As Canada steps into the 21st century, the spirit of the early reformers has not been lost. When education and health care are threatened by shrinking budgets, reformers are sponsoring media campaigns and speaking with politicians and "ordinary" Canadians to make sure that their viewpoints are being heard. Local issues are no longer the only concerns of Canadian reformers. As the world becomes a smaller place, reformers agitate for economic, social, and political change on a global stage. Inclusion, safety, and more equitable standards of living for all members of the world community are now the goals.

Labour and Social Reform is an extensive multi-faceted topic, impossible to cover completely in any one publication. This book introduces major reform themes by focusing on pivotal events and representative issues. It is not an exhaustive examination; rather it is an attempt to provide a starting point for future study. Students will find, for example, that many of the social and labour issues are covered, from different perspectives, in other books in this series. It is an aim of the book to encourage young active citizens. As the early reformers consistently demonstrated, it only takes one person to begin the march of change.

Miriam Bardswich and Sandra Fryer

1872

John A. Macdonald introduces
Trade Unions Act allowing
workers to band together

1872

15 May: Nine Hour Movement,
1500 strikers march through
Hamilton, Ontario

BY 1900, CANADA WAS ENJOYING a period of relative prosperity. The depression that had limited Canada's economic growth and western expansion was over. Prime Minister Wilfrid Laurier's immigration campaign was working and the economy was expanding due to the many newly discovered resource sector developments in the North and new manufacturing plants in cities. Opportunities abounded for enterprising, hardworking individuals who wanted to take advantage of the resources Canada had to offer.

However, despite their willingness to work hard, there were many who had difficulty paying their bills, who lived in poor conditions, who were exploited by their employers, who faced discrimination, or who simply lived in the "wrong" region of the country. The reformers had plenty to do.

In the 1870s, craft unions in the East formed Nine Hour Leagues to reduce the work day by two to three hours. While the movement was unsuccessful in its stated goal, it did bring about significant changes, including the legalization of unions. The Nine Hour Movement was the beginnings of labour solidarity that eventually led to the founding of the Canadian Labour Union, a forerunner to the Trades and Labour Congress of Canada. The idea that working class views could be expressed at the polls was made clear when a printer, Daniel J. O'Donohue, was elected to the Ontario Legislature as an Independent Labour candidate in 1874.

As the first decade of the 20th century drew to a close, long, violent strikes by coal miners took place. In both British Columbia and Cape Breton, Nova Scotia, the government used the army to help the mine owners break the strikes. The strike in Cape Breton ended in complete failure for the miners after ten months on the picket line. In British Columbia, while the United Mine Workers of America won the right to represent the workers, the miners won little else. These and other labour developments across the country led Prime Minister Wilfrid Laurier to recognize the role that labour would play in the future. On 15 May 1909, the Labour Department Act created a separate Labour Portfolio with William Lyon Mackenzie King as its first Minister of Labour.

Changes also took place in other areas of Canadian society. Humane Societies were established to protect children and animals. Children's Aid Societies were formed to look after children who were not being properly cared for. City councils started providing facilities for children's leisure like free swimming pools, public libraries, and establishing separate departments responsible for building and maintaining parks and playgrounds.

Soldiers awaiting orders at the Street Car Strike in Winnipeg, 30 March 1900. Government and industry owners used military intervention in labour disturbances to force workers to end their job actions and further union activity.

"…Just after adjourning the meeting this afternoon the foreman of the Inglis shop, R. Goods, came to the hall and informed us that he had discharged all the scabs in his shop and that he wanted the union men in on Monday, that the firm was tired of the scabs and was willing to give the nine hours…"

— J.H. Barnett, Toronto Iron Moulders International Union secretary, describing one struggle in the Nine Hour Movement, 1903

"A HARD HAND TO BEAT"

NO IRISH NEED APPLY

A common sign at workplaces.

INDUSTRIAL DISPUTES BY CAUSES, 1901-1915		
	Number of Employees Affected	Time Lost in Working Days
For increase in wage............................	142 205	2 732 562
For recognition of union	30 989	2 330 411
For increase in wages and other changes	29 611	2 012 133
For increase in wages and shorter hours	30 281	602 144
Against reduction in wages	28 589	587 418
Against discharge of employees	16 120	335 636
Sympathetic disputes	12 359	331 581
Against employment of nonunionists	20 975	300 045
For shorter hours	8 435	204 274
Against employment of particular persons	6 843	62 321
Unclassified	50 827	1 213 737

Let no union men be weakened
By newspapers' false reports;
Be like sailors on the ocean,
Trusting in their safe lifeboats.
Let your lifeboat be Jehovah
Those who trust Him never fail.
Keep your hand upon the dollar
*And your eyes upon the scale.**

— Excerpt from "Miner's Lifeguard" (aka "A Miner's Life") c.1900-1910

* "keep your eyes upon the scale" refers to the mine owners' practice of under-weighing the miners' coal cars before the unions succeeded in appointing a union man to check weights.

(Beaton Institute/Joe Beaton Collection 91-903-22563)

Iron workers in the Dominion Iron and Steel Company blast furnace, Sydney, N.S., c.1902. Many skilled black steel and iron workers migrated to Cape Breton from the U.S. between 1901-04. They joined other blacks (business people, labourers, and single women) from the U.S. who were looking for better opportunities. They established a community with a church, a school, and recreation facilities. A lack of housing and employment led most to leave Cape Breton by 1905.

STAND FOR A WHITE CANADA

Above: Sign displayed by the Asiatic Exclusion League, which was backed by the Trades and Labour Congress. In September 1907, violent riots against Orientals broke out in Vancouver, with Orientals being beaten and their property damaged.

CHINESE HEAD TAX

In 1907, a petition was circulated among upper class women to repeal the $500 Chinese Head Tax because it contributed to a scarcity of servants in the city. In the VTLC's response to this petition, the importance of race is central to the definition of the working class:

> Thus we urge the present Government to disregard the petition of those ladies of British Columbia, who want Chinese servants. The women of the working class do their own work and when they need help, they employ their own race. Let these ladies who now waste their time…[in] useless functions emulate the example of their poorer sisters and do a little of their own domestic work. If, however, they claim immunity from work, let them pay the price, or modify the conditions of service in such a manner as will secure for them girls of their own race….

— Vancouver Trades and Labour Council, Council Minutes, 21 March 1907

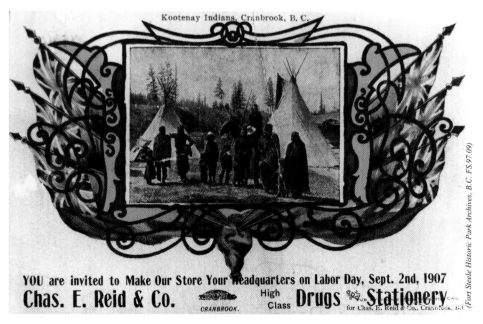

Kootenay Indians, Cranbrook, B.C.

YOU are invited to Make Our Store Your Headquarters on Labor Day, Sept. 2nd, 1907
Chas. E. Reid & Co. CRANBROOK. High Class **Drugs** and **Stationery** for Chas. E. Reid & Co., Cranbrook, B.C.

(Fort Steele Historic Park Archives, B.C. FS.97.09)

Above: Drugstore postcard featuring Kootenay Indians,1907. Although the passage below describes an active, self-sufficient people in 1900, Kootenay participation in the work force was reduced to posing for postcards only a few years later.

"I was agreeably surprised to find that the Kootenays were a tribe practically untouched by the baneful influence of civilization. They had no reservation. They had no agents over them. They received no assistance from the government. They lived entirely upon the production of their rivers, lakes, and forests. They kept strictly to themselves and they never left their beautiful, mountain-girt home. They were peaceful and they had been won over to the Roman Catholic religion by missionaries who had dwelt in their midst since 1842. The Kootenays' independence ended soon after my first visit (1884) when an agent was appointed and reserves given to them..."

— William A. Baillie-Grohman, Kootenay pioneer and speculator, 1900

CHILD LABOUR

Poor city children, Toronto, 1908.

During the 19th century, children were particularly susceptible to abuse in factories and work camps. Although the law did not allow girls under 12 and boys under 14 to work in industry, many did – and for a fraction of the standard wages.

— Museum of Civilization

PRISONS

Opened in 1906, Edmonton's federal penitentiary served as the holding place for outlaws and criminals for 15 years. In 1924 the building became a warehouse.

The Parole and Indefinite Sentence System

...To strengthen the repressive action and at the same time introduce more humanity into the operation of our laws – to sometimes ask for indulgence rather than rigour, without abandoning any of the indispensable guarantees of social order and of justice – is the paramount principle and practical object of the Parole System of Canada.

— Salvation Army Brigadier Walter Archibald, *Canadian Municipal Journal 1908*

Individuals must be sacrificed for the sake of the general object of keeping children out of the mills and factories. If we make the exception we break down the whole law. We do not have the chance to to enforce a law in the cases where it meets with our approval, and let it go in the cases where it works hardship.

— Robert Glocking, head of Ontario Bureau of Labour, in its first Annual Report, February 1901

"The whole dependence of every poor family in the town for fuel is upon the Dog, and...an order to exterminate the dogs was tantamount to an instruction to exterminate the poor."

— Speech by Parsons, MP, Assembly Debate, 19 April 1866

Poor families in the early 1900s still depended on the dog as their work animal.

"My Mum and Dad were struggling. They had 12 kids and Dad couldn't find work because he was a British immigrant. Lots of prejudice against the British then (1909), employers were afraid of union organizers. All of us kids got jobs, me included. I made a wagon from bits of wood I found on the street and used it to deliver meat on Fridays after school and Saturday nights. I was eight.

My route stretched over 20 km. On Saturday nights I'd be gone after an early dinner and often got home around midnight. We couldn't afford gloves or proper boots in the winter...I believe that contributed to my arthritis. But we had to do it until Dad found work and even after he eventually joined Massey-Harris as a tool and dye maker."

— 82-year-old Norman Fryer recalls his early life in Toronto, as told to S. Fryer, 2002

WOMEN IN ACTION

The YWCA's Ontario House, 1900. Black women started organizing to provide shelter for homeless black women when other services discriminated against them and turned them away.

1905	1906	1907	1908	1909
Industrial Workers of the World (IWW) founded	Sunday becomes a day off; Lethbridge coalfield strike	Sept: Riots against Orientals in Vancouver, B.C.	Juvenile Delinquency Act passed	Potlatch ban effectively enforced for the first time in British Columbia

1900
–
1909

SCHOOL CURRICULUMS, PUBLIC AND RESIDENTIAL SCHOOLS 1890-1910

PROGRAMME FOR REGULAR SECONDARY SCHOOLS

reading
writing
grammar
composition
literature
Latin
Greek
French
German
arithmetic
algebra
geometry
trigonometry
chemistry
physics
biology
geography
agricultural science
history — ancient
— British
— Canadian
— general
art
physical training
manual training
household science
commercial subjects
technical subjects

— from C.E. Phillips, *The Development of Education in Canada*

PROGRAMME OF STUDIES FOR INDIAN SCHOOL ETHICS:

Standard I: The practice of cleanliness, obedience, respect, order, neatness.
Standard II: Right and wrong. Truth. Continuance of proper appearance and behaviour.
Standard III: Independence. Self-Respect. Develop the reasons for proper appearance and behaviour.
Standard IV: Industry. Honesty. Thrift.
Standard V: Citizenship of Indians. Patriotism. Industry. Thrift. Self-maintenance. Charity. Pauperism
Standard VI: Indian and white life. Patriotism. Evils of Indian isolation. Enfranchisement. Labour the law of life. Relations of the sexes as to labour. Home and Public Duties.

— Department of Indian Affairs, "Table of a Programme of Studies for Indian Schools," *Annual Report 1896*

The tables show the curriculum for public schools (left) and residential/industrial schools for Aboriginals (right). In hopes of assimilating them into mainstream society and providing them with a "Canadian" education, Aboriginal children were removed from their homes and placed in government and church sponsored residential schools.

HEALTH CARE

(Bloorview MacMillan Children's Centre)

Young patients at the Bloorview MacMillan Centre, Toronto, 1901. In 1899, a group of socially conscious and financially privileged women in Toronto established the Home to care for chronically ill and physically disabled children.

Right: In 1897, Lady Aberdeen, wife of the Governor General of Canada, founded the Victorian Order of Nurses, "…for the nursing of the sick who are otherwise unable to obtain trained nursing in their own homes…[and] to assist in providing small Cottage Hospitals or Homes…"

— *The Victorian Order of Nurses For Canada: 50th Anniversary, 1897-1947*

"If Canada is to become in any real sense a nation, if our people are to become one people, we must have one language. …Hence the necessity of national schools where the teaching of English — our national language — is compulsory. The public school is the most important factor in transforming the foreigners into Canadians."

— J.S. Woodsworth, 1905

In British Columbia, Governor James Douglas advocated the establishment of schools to provide "moral and religious training and a good sound English education."

— Letter from Douglas Barclay, 8 October 1851

I'm killing myself for 10 ¢?

Graffiti chalked on an ore car at the Bell Island Mine, Newfoundland, 1900.

(CTA)

This picture shows the evil of the public drinking cups. We have to give Dr. Hastings, M.H.O., credit for the efforts he has made to abolish this filthy practice. Many cities in Canada should follow the advice of the Toronto's M.H.O. and make the use of the drinking cup a criminal offence.

THE SECOND DECADE of the 20th century opened with optimism, with continued demands for social and labour reform, but also with concrete signs of change. It ended with a country reeling from the losses of World War I and the Spanish Flu epidemic. Over 60 000 died in the Great War and tens of thousands more died from influenza in 1918-19.

As early as 1910 cities began to develop sewer systems, pave roads, build public hospitals, and expand the public school system. Much of the change came as a result of middle class women reformers. They sought improvements in public health codes and hospitals, in education and child protection legislation. They campaigned for safer factories, prison reform, old age pensions, prohibition, and equality for women. Success came in a number of areas: the Dower Act, which recognized common property in marriage; the first federal Department of Public Health; prohibition laws which outlawed the sale of alcoholic beverages; mothers' allowances, and child labour laws.

During the war, women took on non-traditional jobs while the men were overseas. Leading reformers such as Emily Murphy and Nellie McClung used their gifts as writers and speakers to campaign for the franchise. On 27 January 1916, the Bill for the Enfranchisement of Women was passed unanimously by the Manitoba Legislature. Other provinces, with the exception of Quebec, shortly followed and women received the right to vote in federal elections in 1918. Women in Quebec had to wait until 1940 to vote in their own province and aboriginal people would wait until the 1960s.

On the labour front, workers faced unsafe working conditions with few protections. While all provinces except Prince Edward Island had some form of workers' safety laws and compensation for workplace injuries by 1911, none were effective. No province had more than a few safety inspectors. All relied on the courts to determine fault and compensation rates. Then in 1915, Ontario became the first province to establish a government-run workers' compensation system.

As men returned from war and munitions factories closed, jobs were hard to find and labour discontent grew. In Winnipeg in May of 1919, it erupted in a general strike that crippled the city. Three levels of government worked to defeat the strikers: firing strikers, calling in the army, replacing the city police with "special constables" recruited by the anti-strike "Citizens' Committee," threatening to deport foreign-born strikers, and jailing the strike leaders on charges of sedition. The strike ended on 21 June with a crushing defeat for the labour movement as a whole. Nevertheless, many regard the Winnipeg General Strike as a turning point in Canadian labour history.

(CTA. Fonds 1244, Item 343)

The Reciprocity Agreement with the U.S. proposed free trade in natural products and selected semi- and fully-manufactured articles, as well as reciprocal tariff reductions on other goods. Faced with strong opposition to the Agreement, Prime Minister Wilfrid Laurier dissolved Parliament and called an election. The Conservatives warned that free trade would mean an American takeover of Canada. They swept into power with a resounding victory. A headline from 23 September 1911 says it all: "Conservatives Sweep Country; Reciprocity Killed."

The Workmen's Compensation Act
Ontario

Workmen injured by accident in their employment are entitled to first aid or necessary medical aid, and, if disabled from work for seven days or more, to compensation.

THE WORKMAN is required to---
Notify the employer at once of the injury;
Ask for first aid, where proper;
Arrange with employer for medical aid if necessary;
Have report forms received from Board promptly attended to.

THE EMPLOYER is required to---
Notify the Board within three days of every accident disabling a workman or necessitating medical aid;
Provide first aid according to the regulations;
Assist in arranging for a doctor where necessary;
Provide ambulance or transportation to doctor, home, or hospital, where necessary;
Furnish the Board promptly with reports and information as prescribed or requested.

Any workman entitled to compensation who does not receive claim forms promptly, should write the Board.
Legal assistance is not necessary.
The workman is not to pay the doctor for services or reports under the Act.
In fatal accidents the workman's dependants are entitled to compensation.
For further information or for copies or synopsis of the Act write the Board.

THE WORKMEN'S COMPENSATION BOARD
66 TEMPERANCE STREET, TORONTO, ONT.

Employers are required under the Act to keep this Poster posted up within easy access of all their workmen.

WORKMEN'S COMPENSATION ACT POSTER

1911	1913	1913	1914
27 May: Strike by Springhill coal miners ends after 22 months – miners fail to gain union recognition	Introduction of the assembly line by Ford Motor Company	Miners riot in B.C., protesting the hiring of Orientals as strike-breakers	Canada's first Workmen's Compensation Board is formed in Ontario

1910 – 1919

Lethbridge Herald 1914:
Typical monthly budget for an average family of five:

Groceries	$20
Butcher	$10
Baker	$ 4
Coal	$ 5
Light	$ 1.50
Water	$ 1.50
Rent	$15 (five-room cottage)
Clothing	$20
Druggist	$ 2
Doctor	$ 2 (average over 5 years)
Incidental	$ 5
Total	$86 ($1,032 a year)

EDUCATION AND CHILD LABOUR

(NAC C-70945)

(Edith S. Watson)

Left: This 14-year-old coal miner was typical of children forced into hard labour to help support their families. Right: The boys' side of the class, c.1910, Shippegan Island, NB. Child labour was common in the early 20th century. Reformers attempted to change this by pressing for compulsory education. By 1911, 85% of all children between ages 10 and 12 were in school. However, large numbers of children from Britain were still being recruited as farm labourers well into the 1920s and it was not until 1929 that children were legally excluded from factory and mine employment.

Until a comparatively recent period the schools were organized on purely academic lines and the avowed aim of education was culture and discipline. This aim has, however, been greatly enlarged within the past few years, by including within its scope the development of a sense of social and civic duty, the stimulation of national and patriotic spirit, the promotions of public health, and direct preparations for the occupations of life.

— Manitoba Association for School Principals, 1913

A child in a Toronto slum, 1913. Urban reformers struggled to clean up slums and worked towards improved public education.

Sewers come to Toronto, 1910. Urban reform advanced dramatically in this decade.

(CTA Series 372, Sub-series 32, Item 297)

Posters at the Canadian National Exhibition advocating child care, August 1914.

WOMEN IN ACTION

"Among the people of the world in the years to come, we will ask no greater heritage for our country than to be known as the land of the Fair Deal, where no person can "exert influence" to bring about his personal ends; where no man or woman's past can ever rise up to defeat them; where no crime goes unpunished; where every debt is paid; where no prejudice is allowed to masquerade as a reason; where honest toil will insure an honest living; where the man who works receives the reward of his labour."

— Nellie McClung, 1915

(NAC C-27674)

Decades of campaigning by activists such as (from left) Nellie McClung, Alice Jamieson, and Emily Murphy won for women recognition as "persons" and the right to vote.

"Being a fairly able-bodied woman, I would prefer to open the carriage door myself and be given a fair deal in the laws of my country and the right to vote for such changes in those laws as I happen to see fit."

— Francis Marion Beynon, 1913

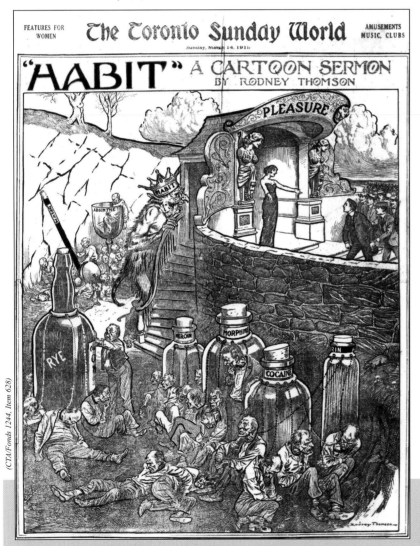

(CTA/Fonds 1244, Item 628)

In the late 19th century, women's groups like the Women's Christian Temperance Union fought for Prohibition in Canada. By the end of 1916, Alberta, Manitoba, and Saskatchewan had passed Prohibition legislation making it illegal to sell alcohol. By 1917, all other provinces except Quebec endorsed Prohibition. In 1918, the Dominion government used the War Measures Act to apply Prohibition to Quebec. Most provinces ended Prohibition in the 1920s.

WOMEN'S CHRISTIAN TEMPERANCE UNION
(White Ribboners)

The Second Public Annual Meeting of the above Society will be held (D.V.) in the

St. Paul's Methodist Church
12th Street, HILLHURST

ON FRIDAY, MARCH 6th, 1914

(Glenbow NA-2629-19)

LIQUOR ENSLAVES, PROHIBITION SETS FREE!
The last to be hired, the first to be fired, is the man who drinks!

— Women's Christian Temperance Union slogans

TOUCH NOT. TASTE NOT. HANDLE NOT.

◦ PLEDGE ◦

I hereby promise, by the help of God, to abstain from the use of all intoxicating liquors, including wine, beer, and cider, as a beverage, from the use of tobacco in any form, and from all profanity.

The Woman's Christian Temperance Union's "Triple Pledge."

A person addicted to its habitual use is known as a cocainist...The general rule is that addiction is present mainly in youths from 16 to 21 years of age. Narcotics hinder development, and boys and girls are forever wrecked. Distracted parents come pleading for aid and advice. The complaint is always the same – 'If we only knew the first sign of this dreadful curse we could have saved the boy.'

— Magistrate Emily F. Murphy, "Fighting Drugs," *Maclean's*, 15 February 1920

NUMBER OF HOURS OF WORK NEEDED TO PAY FOR BASIC COMMODITIES IN HAMILTON: 1911 AND 1920

	Hourly Wage		Month's Rent		Ton Coal		1 lb Coffee		1 lb Flour		1 lb Butter		1 lb Sirloin	
	1911	1920	1911	1920	1911	1920	1911	1920	1911	1920	1911	1920	1911	1920
Bricklayers	.50	1.03	30	25	13.5	14	.7	.5	.06	.07	.5	.6	.4	.4
Carpenters	.40	.85	37.5	30	16.9	17	.9	.6	.07	.08	.6	.7	.5	.5
Sheet-Metal Workers	.35	.85	42.9	30	19.3	17	1	.6	.08	.08	.7	.7	.5	.5
Machinists	.32$\frac{1}{2}$	.73	46	36	20.8	20	1.1	.7	.09	.1	.7	.8	.6	.6
Bldg. Labourers	.27$\frac{1}{2}$	.55	54.5	47	24.5	26	1.3	.9	.11	.1	.9	1.0	.7	.7
Factory Labourers	.17	.41	88	63	40	35	2	1.2	.18	.13	1.4	1.1	1.1	.7

(Compiled from monthly figures in Labour Gazette, 1911-1920, and in Canada Dept. of Labour, Wages and Hours of Labour in Canada, 1901-1920 [Ottawa 1921])

1910 – 1919

The Industrial Workers of the World (IWW) or "Wobblies," founded in 1905, had both American and Canadian workers as members. The union saw itself as a democratically-run organization that wished to organize all workers into one big union. Others saw its members as anarchists.

(NAC C-18734)

(NAC PA-24562)

Industrial workers at home were as vital to the war effort as were soldiers overseas.
Left: Women eagerly took on non-traditional jobs such as this tough and dangerous work in a munitions factory (1915-17) to help with the war effort.
Right: A worker loads a cartridge case at the Energite Explosives Co. Ltd., Renfrew, Ontario.

SPANISH FLU EPIDEMIC

Right: Nurses in High River, Alberta, wear face masks to protect against the Spanish Flu virus. Soldiers returning from World War I in the spring of 1918 brought with them the Spanish Flu. The flu spread like wild fire across the country, killing over 30 000.

(Glenbow NA-3452-2)

The Victorian Order of Nurses (VON) was one of many organizations that pitched in to help during the epidemic. The following are extracts from the VON Annual Report of 1918:

Towards the end of October the epidemic started to become serious and the Y.M.C.A. was opened as a temporary hospital, and the upper rooms of the Town Hall were set aside for the care of children…we had 53 deaths in Cobalt – there were…500 cases. — Cobalt, Ontario

The Spanish Influenza paralyzed everything…all places of business were practically at a standstill while the malady was raging. The doctor was down with it, but our nurse showed splendid spirit and rose to the occasion… — Quesnel, B.C.

A Turning Point for Labour: THE WINNIPEG GENERAL STRIKE

Winnipeg General Strike Timeline

1 May: Metal workers go on strike for a 44-hour week (in place of 60-hours) and 85 cents per hour wage scale.

15 May: The Trades and Labour Congress calls a General Strike in Winnipeg, demanding decent wages, an eight-hour day, and collective bargaining. Private businesses, factories, public services (except for railroads) cut off as 30 000 workers walk off their job.

17 June: Federal government arrests leaders of strike; 10 labour leaders charged with sedition and conspiracy against the Dominion of Canada. Three eventually jailed (and later win election to Manitoba legislature while in jail).

21 June: Bloody Saturday – mounted police charge crowd of peaceful demonstrators, killing 2 and wounding dozens.

25 June: With its leaders facing trial, its members hungry and penniless, the Winnipeg Trades and Labour Congress surrenders and the Strike ends.

Greater Winnipeg Veterans Association demonstration at City Hall, 4 June 1919. Some members of the GWVA and the Imperial Veterans in Canada had claimed that organized labour was "violating law and order." The strikers response was that the strike had "... been in progress for two weeks [and]...not one case of disorderly conduct [had] been reported."

Modern industrial society is divided into two classes, those who possess and do not produce, and those who produce and do not possess.

— Constitution of One Big Union, March 1919

Mayor's Position:

As mayor of this city, by the suffrage of the people, I wish to state most emphatically that I will not allow myself to be stampeded by any particular section of society, but will act and will only act as the occasion warrants in the interests of the people...

Citizens, go about your business quietly.

Do not congregate in crowds.

Make no provocative statements.

And at all times realize that the constituted authorities will take all the necessary steps to ensure no radical departure from the normal, law-abiding conditions of community life.

— Mayor of Winnipeg, *Manitoba Free Press*, 1 May 1919

CRUSH IT.   (Mail & Empire)

Views of the Citizens Committee:

[The strike] is a serious attempt to overturn British institutions in this western country and to supplant them with the Russian Bolshevik system of Soviet rule...Why is it that one finds many thousands of men and women among the strikers who state quite frankly that they had no wish to strike – that they did not want to strike, and yet, paradoxically, they are on strike?

It is because the "Red" element in Winnipeg has assumed the ascendancy in the labour movement, dominating and influencing – or stampeding – the decent element of that movement, which desires the preservation of British institutions, yet is now striking unconsciously against them...

— *Winnipeg Citizen* (published by the Citizens' Committee of the employers), 17 May 1919

Fearful of the One Big Union, a movement formed in 1917, and a possible "Bolshevik revolution," citizens, the media, and government turned on the strikers. Businessmen claimed the strike would decide whether "the Union Jack or the Red Flag will prevail."

1919

17 June: The government arrests
ten leaders of the Winnipeg Strike

1919

21 June: "Bloody Saturday"
RCMP attack protesters

1920-1

Four Winnipeg Strike leaders (3 still in prison) are elected to
Manitoba Provincial Legislature; J.S. Woodsworth, a strike
leader, is elected to Parliament as a labour representative

1910
—
1919

(CTA/Fonds 1244, Item 2543)

Striker's viewpoint:

...this strike will continue until it extends from Halifax to Victoria....We have withdrawn labour from all industry, and it will stay withdrawn until the bosses realize that they cannot stand against the masses of labour. If we can control industrial production now, at this time, we can control it for all time to come, and we can control the Government of this country, too.

— Ernest Robinson, one of the leaders of the Winnipeg Strike, *Manitoba Free Press*, 20 May 1919

(Provincial Archives of Manitoba N12316)

Above: Bloody Saturday, 21 June 1919. Mounties charge the workers' demonstration and open fire after the strikers throw rocks and sticks.

Political Comment:

It is too much for me to say that the vast number of intelligent residents who went on strike were seditious or that they were either dull enough or weak enough to be led by seditionaries...but the cause of the strike...was the specific grievance [*the refusal of collective bargaining*]...and the dissatisfied and unsettled conditions of Labour at and long before the beginning of the strike.

...it is more likely that the cause of the strike is...[*other than unemployment*], the high cost of living, inadequate wages...profiteering...

— H.A. Robson, *The Report of Commission to Enquire into the Causes and Effects of the General Strike*, November 1919

The strike has been entirely misrepresented. I know the details intimately. Without hesitation I say that there was not a single foreigner in a position of leadership, though foreigners were falsely arrested to give colour to this charge...

In short, it was the biggest hoax that was ever "put over" any people! Government officials and the press were largely responsible...

— J.S. Woodsworth, in a letter to a cousin, 21 August 1921
Woodsworth was charged along with other strike leaders and acquitted. He was elected to the federal Parliament in 1921.

15

1920 - 1929

1921
Agnes Macphail – first
woman elected to House
of Commons

1922
12 000 coal miners in
B.C. and Alberta strike
for six months

1924
First national posta
strike; end of
Prohibition in Alber

THE "ROARING TWENTIES" is a term that suggests prosperity and conjures up images of flappers, jazz, rum-runners, daring bush pilots, radios, and automobiles. However, the "roar" was much louder in the U.S. than it was in Canada. Although British Columbia, Ontario, and part of the prairies enjoyed prosperity during the last half of the decade, there were many social, labour, and regional problems. According to a 1929 Department of Labour report, over 70% of working people earned less than $1 000 a year. In Quebec, industrialization lagged behind Ontario. The Palliser Triangle of southern Alberta and Saskatchewan endured a devastating drought that drove people from the area long before the "Dirty Thirties." Maritimers felt increasingly alienated as they faced high unemployment and young people left for Ontario or the eastern United States. On the labour front, wage cutting was widespread; union membership was in decline; and the labour movement was increasingly divided, with church-controlled Catholic unions developing in Quebec and Communists gaining support within traditional unions. Lengthy strikes were common, especially in the Cape Breton coal fields and steel mills in 1922, 1923, and 1925. Again, private company "police" and the Canadian Army were sent in to combat the strikers.

On the positive side, the 1920s saw the introduction of social reforms and the promise of labour change. The Old Age Pensions Act was introduced in 1927. Minimum wage laws were passed in more provinces, although most still did not include women. The International Labour Organization, of which Canada was a member, vowed to work for better wages and working conditions, including an eight-hour day. Leaders of the Winnipeg General Strike, J.S. Woodsworth and A.A. Heaps, were elected to the House of Commons as labour representatives. Social reformer Agnes Macphail became the first woman MP. In 1929, after a long campaign by the "Famous Five," Britain's Privy Council recognized women as "persons" making them eligible to be appointed senators and judges.

In the West, farmers formed cooperatives called Wheat Pools. These cooperatives brought stability to the marketing and sale of wheat. In the East, Reverend Moses Coady and Father "Jimmy" Tompkins founded the Antigonish Movement, a unique program of adult education and cooperation, centred at St. Francis Xavier University. Today's cooperatives and credit unions trace their roots to these movements. Meanwhile, the Maritime Rights Movement won expanded port facilities and lower freight rates.

The 1920s ended with the stock market crash in October of 1929, an event that signalled the beginning of the Great Depression of the 1930s.

(Grain Growers Guide, November 1921)

Political Slogans Illustrated:
"PROTECTION CREATES WORK"
(For the Politicians)

STRIKERS AND TROOPERS CLASH *The Sydney Post*, 17 July 1925
The detachment of Royal Canadian Dragoons, which were forwarded here from Sydney last night were met on their arrival by a mob, which attacked the Mounted Men with sticks and stones. The troopers rode through a fusillade of flying missiles, one of which found serious target, a Dragoon being put out of business.

Some of the most bitter labour conflicts in Canada were between the coal miners and steel workers of Cape Breton Island and their employers. In the early 1920s there were frequent strikes, often violent. In a prolonged strike in 1925, over 400 troops arrived in Sydney in mid June to maintain order. On 17 July, they clashed with strikers

THE MILITANT COAL MINERS

The Coal Barons: "Trouble with you people is, you want the earth."
The Coal Miners: "Trouble with you is you've got it."

"A *woman's place is anywhere she wants to be.*"

— Agnes Macphail

On 6 September 1921, 31-year-old Agnes Macphail became the first female member of the Canadian House of Commons. Although her election into Parliament made history, few of the country's newspapers even bothered to interview Macphail. Despite this initial indifference and the hostility she later faced from some of her male colleagues, she enjoyed a long and distinguished political career.

"I believe the preservation of the home in the future lies almost entirely in the hands of men. If they are willing to give women economic freedom in that home, if they are willing to live by the standard they wish women to live by, then home will be the preserve. If the preservation of the home means the enslavement of women, economically or morally, then we had better break it."

— Agnes Macphail

One of the greatest difficulties in the way of closer and more friendly relations between Capital and Labor in Canada is the fact that the great bulk of our organized labor has its membership in American unions…The great majority of their membership is American, their central officers are all American, their funds are paid into, and are controlled from, American head offices, and these same American head offices control the policies of the Canadian minority members.

Such an arrangement is becoming more and more obnoxious to all thinking Canadians. American labor has no intimate knowledge of, or sympathy with, or part in, our natural schemes of nationhood and should have no voice in our industrial life.

I am not a "Red." I believe in the principle of collective bargaining. But the desired co-operation between Capital and Labor will never be realized to any appreciable degree until Canadian workers assert their right and determination to govern their own affairs.

— Roland Lamberthe, *Union Labor at the Cross-roads,* 1 November 1921

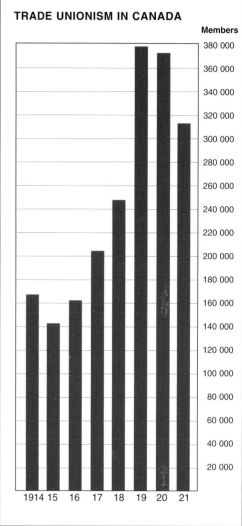

TRADE UNIONISM IN CANADA

(Labour Organizations in Canada, 1924-26)

1920 – 1929

ISLAND CRISIS

His name was Eddie Crimmins
And he came from Port aux Basques,
Besides a chance to live and work
He had nothing much to ask...
And yet, he starved, he starved, I tell you,
Back in nineteen twenty-four,
And before he died he suffered
As many have before.
When the mines closed down that winter
He had nothing left to eat,
And he starved, he starved, I tell you,
On your dirty, damned street.

— Dawn Fraser, *Echoes From Labor's Wars,* 1926

Right: *Glace Bay* by Lawren Harris, c.1921. This stark block print of a woman and her family in the Glace Bay mining town of Cape Breton, Nova Scotia, reflects the despair felt by many Maritimers as they faced mass unemployment, extended strikes and horrific poverty. In this work of "social realism" the artist has become social activist.

(AGO/NC-1681)

1930 - 1939

1930
Canada is in Depression;
22 Sept: Unemployment Relief Act
is passed by Parliament

1931
11 Aug: Eight Communist leaders
including Tim Buck are arrested
for "unlawful association"

THE GREAT DEPRESSION of the 1930s was the worst economic downturn of the 20th century. Unemployment hit record highs; people lost their farms, their homes, their life savings, and their future prospects. Uncertainty and discontent found expression in labour and social protests, and in new political parties.

People with money lived well as prices fell, but most people endured hard times. As trade declined, factories, mines, and other businesses closed, throwing thousands out of work while wages for those still working fell dramatically. Many young men, even some women, "rode the rods" searching for work that didn't exist, begging for food, and sleeping in "hobo jungles" near the railway lines. Others took jobs in remote relief camps, earning twenty cents a day for back breaking work. Thousands of relief camp workers went on strike in 1935 and began the On-to-Ottawa Trek to protest conditions. The trek ended when protesters clashed with police in the Regina Market Square and two people were killed.

Traditional craft unions could do little. A new kind of organization, the industrial union which organized all the workers in a company, was on the rise. A strike by coal miners in Estevan, Saskatchewan, in 1931 ended with the deaths of three miners. In 1937, General Motors workers in Oshawa, Ontario, joined the United Auto Workers after the fifth pay cut in five years. Their strike was a major victory for the new labour organization, the Committee for Industrial Organization (CIO). Later, Algoma Steelworkers in Sault Ste. Marie, succeeded in gaining a 44-hour week, union recognition, and a payroll check off of union dues.

Prime Minister Bennett was unable to ease unemployment and the farm crisis. His attempt to introduce unemployment insurance failed and other policies of his version of Roosevelt's popular "New Deal" seemed to be "too little too late." Some people turned to radical politics such as Communism and Fascism. Communist leaders like Tim Buck were arrested for belonging to "unlawful associations." Protests against the violation of civil rights grew, but so did prejudice against "foreigners."

Two new parties emerged in the West. In Alberta, William Aberhart created the right-wing Social Credit Party which was elected in 1935. Farmers, unionists, social gospel preachers, and socialists from across Canada joined to form the left-wing Cooperative Commonwealth Federation (CCF). Its Regina Manifesto proposed public control of banks, minimum wage laws, and national health care. Although the CCF remained a third party, many of the policies advocated gradually came into effect.

The poverty and the hopelessness of the Depression affected people for decades. But, it also proved the need for labour unions and social reform.

SIGNS OF THE TIMES

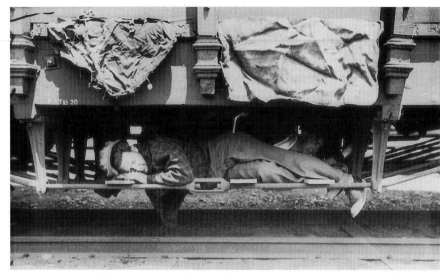

"Riding the Rods," thousands of jobless men and some women hitched rides on freight trains travelling across the country in search of work.

A victim of the Depression finds that no work means no home. He protests against lack of public relief while he sleeps on a cot set up for the homeless in an office.

Brother, Can You Spare A Dime?

They used to tell me I was building a dream
And so I followed the mob
When there was earth to plow or guns to bear
I was always there right on the job

They used to tell me I was building a dream
With peace and glory ahead
Why should I be standing in line
Just waiting for bread?

Once I built a railroad, I made it run
Made it race against time
Once I built a railroad, now it's done
Brother, can you spare a dime?

(Gorney, Harburg)
No song captures the dark spirit of the Great Depression better than this 1932 hit song, which was written for a Broadway musical, and went to #1 on the charts.

(E.A-160-1231)

Children at a May Day demonstration, 1 May 1937. May Day is an international holiday honouring workers.

(McMaster Labour Studies)

Above: Controller Sam Lawrence pickets in support of the 9-hour day for restaurant workers, Hamilton, Ontario c.1930

(NAC PA-129184)

Left: Women marching against Duplessis' Padlock Law, Montreal, January 1939. This law allowed the closing of any building used for "propagating Communism or Bolshevism." Since the law did not define "Communist" or "Bolshevist," it could and was used against anyone that the Duplessis government thought was "subversive," such as labour unionists and Jehovah Witnesses. Twenty years later, the Supreme Court of Canada declared the law unconstitutional.

Estevan Mercury, 1 October 1931

Death and Destruction Ride Rampant

The staccato bark of revolvers, the whine of death-dealing bullets, the dull thud of flying missiles as they rained about the heads and shoulders of police officers, the guttural rumble of an angry mob, the piercing screams of wildly excited women and the hoarse shouts of men in bitter battle, these shattered the peace and quiet of a beautiful autumn afternoon Tuesday as tranquil Fourth St. was suddenly transformed into a maelstrom of bloodshed and destruction.... Halted by Royal Canadian Mounted Police when they attempted to parade through Estevan, 400 striking miners and their wives, mobilized from the industrially crippled coalfields, beat back the redcoats with a smashing barrage of rocks, loaded sticks, pieces of steel and iron piping, and chunks of cement, Unable to repulse the attack with their riding crops and batons, the police drew their guns and fired. Two men were killed and a score of people injured during the running fight, which broke up on the arrival of police reinforcements armed with rifles...it was a tragic climax to a labor dispute in which the cause of the workers had been inflamed to the point of open violence by exhortations of outside leaders.

Estevan

Dig, dig,
For the fatted pig.

The story, Estevan, is in your scroll,
In writhing lines of lead and blood and coal.

Copper, pump 'em full of lead!
Slaves with a grudge are better dead.

Dig, dig,
For the fatted pig.

Coal in their blood as they paid the toll.
Give the owner blood in his coal.

Madam wants an exotic feather.
Lead and blood and coal together.

Dig, dig,
For the fatted pig.

— Signed V.G., *Canadian Forum,* March 1932

LIFE DURING THE GREAT DEPRESSION

A mother and child are "out on the street," evicted from their Montreal tenement in 1930.

…Shabby houses jostled one another on either side of narrow streets. Occasionally one found an attempt to beautify the front garden, by coaxing a sparse lawn to grow upon ground which was a mixture of sand, and slag from nearby furnaces, and pitiful beds of geraniums and begonias grew straggly and soon became blackened by soot from neighbouring smokestacks.

(NAC C-30811)

— Description of working class housing appearing in the 1933 novel *Forgotten Men,* set in Hamilton, Ontario

A TYPICAL DAY'S WORK
FOR THE SANITATION INSPECTORS

• Report & sign in at City Hall at 7:50 a.m.

• Turn in previous days[sic] work & get work for day.

• Leave City Hall at 8:30 & go out to district.

• Investigate complaints sent in, re-inspect previous complaints, report on progress of work done. Complaints consist of general inspection of dwelling houses, plumbing & drainage, roofs and eavestroughs, wet cellars, garbage disposal, heating of premises, condition of furnaces, temperature of rooms in cold weather.

— *Activists and Advocates*, Toronto's Health Dept, 1883-1983

Diets for Unemployment Relief
As Approved by Saskatoon Civic Relief Boar
August 31, 1933

One Adult Person.................Diet 8
Man and Wife........................Diet 16
Man and Wife with one Child up to two years of age......Diet 17
Man and Wife with one Child over 2 and under 6 yrs...Diet 17A
For each Child over 6 years and under 12 years of age add 2 diets.

For each Child over 12 years and under 21 years of age add 4 diets.

Widow or Widower and eldest Child—classed.............Diet 16 and other children as set out above.

NUMBER 8 DIET	
Tea, Coffee or Cocoa............	⅛ lb.
Sugar	1 lb.
Butter	½ lb.
Rice, Tapioca, Rolled Oats, Granules or Flour...............2 lbs. or 1 lb. each of any two	

DIET 16	
Tea, Coffee or Cocoa............	¼ lb.
Sugar	2 lbs.
Butter	1 lb.
Rice or Tapioca......................	2 lbs. or 1 lb. sugar or ¼ lb. tea, coffee, cocoa
R Oats Granules or Flour	3 lbs

BACKYARD MINING IN CAPE BRETON

I was a young girl, perhaps fourteen or fifteen. It was the middle of the Depression and the coal mines on Cape Breton Island weren't working full time. One section in a mine near our home, my Dad's mine, had been abandoned. We would mine this section from our backyard.

My father, two of my brothers and I were the miners. We had a shaft over a hundred feet deep and it was drilled out to the worked out area of the mine. My father was still working at his regular job but when he came home he worked in "our mine," at a wall of coal about five feet thick. When my brother Joe was home from college he helped as would brother Anthony who had just finished grade eleven.

My brothers lowered me in a large bucket. I would sit on the edge of the shaft, put my feet in the bucket and hold onto the rope. As I descended those 100 feet I would be swaying back and forth. When I reached the bottom I followed planks to where my father was working. When my Dad filled a bucket of coal I would

take it , in a wheel barrow, to the shaft and climb a ladder to attach it to the rope. Joe or Anthony would raise it to the surface and I would wait below for the empty bucket to return. They needed to stay on the surface because strength was needed to raise the buckets of coal those 100 feet.

It was beautiful, beautiful coal. We sold it, illegally. Trucks came to our gate to pick it up. It was sold door to door in Sydney, at half the price of government coal. The police knew about it and sometimes a truck driver would be arrested.

Our mining was a family affair. But, one day when we went down we found the mine flooded. It was the end of my career. It was impossible to fill in the shaft. We did put old mattresses and things down there and eventually it was sealed.

I didn't mind it at the time, going down that shaft. But later, even after I was married, I would think about it or dream about it. And shiver.

— Nellie, Cape Breton, as told to M. Bardswich, 2002

The March of the "Resoluters"

James Simpson, a vice president of the Trades and Labour Council, led delegates to its convention in Windsor, Ontario in 1933. He wanted the council to endorse the new Cooperative Commonwealth Federation. This cartoon shows how other delegates may have viewed them.

Hamstrung by Politics

Certain of the country's business leaders have privately expressed themselves as being worried by the growth of radical publications in Canada....They have got hold of the wrong end of the stick.

The question to be answered is why are so many people interested in radical ideas? They are not all anarchists or revolutionists. They want security, and security and revolution don't go together. The answer is that for them the old system has broken down.

They cannot get work except in relief camps. They cannot feed and clothe and educate their children. They may get state or municipal charity. But they cannot establish themselves. If they are middle-aged, they may never get a steady job again. A vast army of idle youth is waiting to take the jobs if and when they come.

...Correct their situation and there is no need to worry about them seeing red.

— H. Napier Moore, Editor, *Macleans*, 15 November 1934

James Woodsworth (Winnipeg North Centre): Mr. Speaker, I move:

Whereas the prevalence of the present depression throughout the world indicates fundamental defects in the existing economic system, be it resolved that the government should immediately take measures to the setting up of a cooperative commonwealth in which all natural resources and the socially necessary machinery of production will be used in the interests of the people and not for the benefit of the few.

Mr. Speaker, we must distinguish between the CCF and Communism. It is true that both believe in a changed social order, in a new economic system. The Communists are convinced that this can be brought about only by violence. We believe that it may come in Canada by peaceful methods and in an orderly fashion.

Raymond Morand (Essex East): The end being the same.

Woodsworth: It may very well be that force may prove inevitable, yes, if the attitude of certain gentlemen is persisted in and the people of this country are denied the right they have in self-expression and to the enjoyment of a decent livelihood!

We believe that the first step to be taken in bettering the present conditions is to adopt a planned economy. I do not think we could proceed very far without increasing the public control of industry…I do not believe that the industrialist can pay his dividends today and at the same time pay decent wages. But when that alternative must be decided, I say unhesitatingly that the employees ought to be secured a decent living and their claims should have priority over dividend. If industry as constituted under present conditions cannot grant a decent living to its employees…it should be taken over.

— House of Commons debate, 1 February 1933

(NAC PA-805441)

They Won't Fit Him Very Well

(Winnipeg Free Press)

THE "ON-TO-OTTAWA" TREK

(NAC C-29399)

Trekkers began to join the "On-to-Ottawa" trains in B.C. and others kept joining across the prairies. Many had to travel on top of the cars as they became increasingly crowded.

Hear the Reply of the authorities to Strikers' Delegation requesting immediate Relief and opening of negotiations on counter-proposals to Bennett Government's offer of Concentration Camps

MASS MEETING TONIGHT
Market Square 8 p.m.

(If wet will be held in Stadium)

Several Speakers representing local organizations will address the crowd

Winnipeg Strike Camp situation will be outlined. Latest developments will be given

Strikers' Funds are Completely Depleted

Support the Strikers and Force the authorities to grant immediate Relief

A planned one-day stop at Regina grew into two weeks, and Trek organizers rushed to respond to Prime Minister Bennett's warning that the government would use force to prevent the Trekkers from continuing to Ottawa. This poster advertised the meeting that led to the Regina Riot.

Hold the Fort – The Trekkers' Song
(originally English Transport Workers' Strike Song)

We meet today in Freedom's cause,
And raise our voices high;
We'll join our hands in union strong,
To battle or to die.
Chorus:
Hold the fort for we are coming-
Union men, be strong.
Side by side we battle onward,
Victory will come.

(Saskatchewan Archives R-B 171[3])

The Regina Riot, 1 July 1935. The Canadian Press reported: "For more than two hours violent fighting continued between the camp 'deserters' and police."

The police must have had orders to beat and rout us thoroughly that night, for there can be no other explanation for the senseless continuation of those stupid horse charges.

We were not a rabble. We refused to be beaten up. We had tried desperately to avoid combat, even after the first unprovoked police attack.

— Richard Liversedge, a Trekker's view, from *Recollections of the On-to-Ottawa Trek*

REGINA, JULY 2 – Ominous quiet settled over Regina today after a day of rioting and bloodshed. One man, Plainclothes Detective Charles Miller lay dead, fatally pummelled when caught in the surging melee of an army of relief camp strikers and sympathizers who turned violently upon police as they broke up an open-air meeting in the city's market square.

— *The Ottawa Evening Citizen*, 2 July 1935

1938	1939	1939	1939
Conservationist Grey Owl dies – the secret of his "Iroquois" birth is revealed	Prairie Farm Assistance Act passes	7 June: Jewish refugees arriving in Canada on the *St. Louis* are denied entry to Canada	10 Sept: Canada declares war on Germany

OSHAWA STRIKE

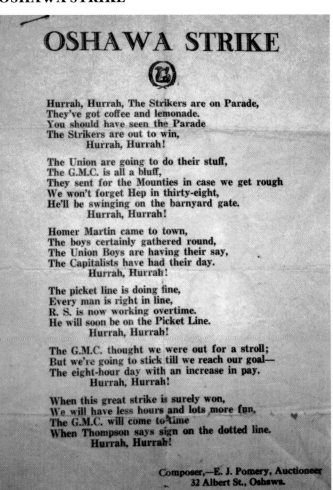

A poster from the United Auto Workers (UAW) during the General Motors strike in Oshawa, Ontario, April 1937. As a result of this strike, the workers won a 44-hour week and a promise of no discrimination against union members.

"…The fifteen day walkout of some four thousand (Oshawa) workers marks the birth of the Canadian labour movement as we know it today."

— Irving Abella

If there is dissatisfaction in Canada as in the United States, it is because we are forced to live in what amounts to peonage and slavery while a great part of productivity has been shifted into the pockets of a relatively few people.

— Homer Martin, International UAW President, *The Toronto Star*, 12 April 1937

20 June 1938, "Bloody Sunday." Police use tear gas against unemployed demonstrators who had occupied the main post office in Vancouver.

EDUCATION

A log-cabin school in Northern Ontario, a railway school car, and a "modern" school building in 1935.

Supporting Public Education in Ontario, 1935: If a school is conducted in accordance with the regulations and reaches the required standard, it receives a grant of money from the provincial government. These grants are largest in the case of schools in the newer and more sparsely settled parts of the country, where the settlers need help the most…. In the cities the greater part of the cost of the schools is met by school taxes levied on the taxpayers; in the outlying parts of the country the greater part of the cost is borne by the provincial government. Where there are no schools, the provincial government tries to fill the want by means of correspondence courses and of railway cars equipped as schools.

— Stewart Wallace, *A Reader in Canadian Civics*, 1935

1940
25 Apr: Quebec women receive the right to vote and run for office in the province

1941
1 July: Unemployment Insurance Act comes into effect

1941
7 Dec: Japanese attack Pearl Harbor; Canada declares war on Japan

BY 1940 THE HARD TIMES of the Depression had been replaced by the challenges of "total war." The War Measures Act enabled the government to mobilize resources — expand the civil service, implement wage and price controls, increase taxes, and create full employment. Once again, women returned to jobs on assembly lines, in shipyards and mines, and on farms. Again, a national day-care system was established that made it possible for women to take those jobs. But they were never paid what men earned and were expected, when the war ended, to return to their traditional roles as stay-at-home mothers or in traditional female jobs.

"Total war" made it easier to enact reforms. Unemployment Insurance was introduced in 1941. The Wartime Housing Corporation built new homes and helped repair and modernize existing ones. Controls were put on rents and the Veterans Land Act of 1942 provided low cost mortgages to service personnel. In 1944, the Family Allowance Act was passed granting a "baby bonus" to all families with children.

Industrial unions continued to organize during the war despite wage controls. Long, bitter strikes were fought in 1941 by miners in Kirkland Lake, Ontario and aluminum workers in Arvida, Quebec. Both strikes were crushed when provincial police and soldiers were sent in to keep up production. The federal government enacted PC 1003 in 1944 to provide the means by which unions could be certified and bargain for their members without having to go on strike. To end the Windsor Ford strike in 1945, Ontario created the Rand Formula, which allowed the deduction of union dues from all employees' paychecks, although no one would be required to join the union.

CIO unions were actively organizing major industries throughout Canada. Forestry workers in B.C., seamen on the Great Lakes, textile workers in Quebec, and steelworkers in Hamilton, all demanded wage increases, eight-hour days, and union certification. The decade ended with the Asbestos Strike which many believe was the real beginning of the "Quiet Revolution" in Quebec.

By the end of the war, Canadian ideas of social reform were being accepted internationally. Even before victory in Europe, Canada was involved with the United Nations Relief and Rehabilitation Administration and would accept over 186 000 of Europe's "displaced persons" by 1952. Canadian ideas about human rights were given international prominence by John Humphrey, a Canadian lawyer who drafted the Universal Declaration of Human Rights and became the first director of the Human Rights Division of the United Nations Secretariat.

HOME FRONT WAR EFFORT

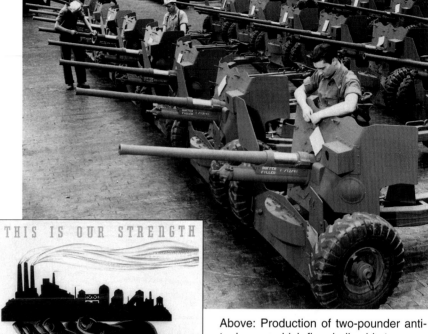

Above: Production of two-pounder anti-tank guns which fire shells able to penetrate tanks or destroy rails

THIS IS OUR STRENGTH

LABOUR and MANAGEMENT are pooling their strength to give us the means for victory in war and progress in peace.

(NAC C-87500)

Right: Five sisters, employed by the Canadian National Railway, pose aboard a train engine in a "V" formation, while holding war bonds.

PC 1003 (Privy Council Order 1003) 1943

In an atmosphere of union - management conflict and several strikes in wartime industries, the federal government, in February 1943, introduced Privy Council Order 1003. Designed to prevent further strikes it recognized the right of unions to organize and forced employers to bargain with the unions in good faith. There were, of course, ways of getting around PC 1003, but, by the end of the war, provinces had included its principles in their labour codes. This was a major gain for the labour movement in Canada.

Above: "Parachute Riggers" was one of a group of paintings by Canadian artist Paraskeva Clark that featured women at work in war industries.

Below: Industrial labour on the Home front was as essential as military action overseas.

(NAC C-89454)

ast and steady speeds my lathe
So Hitler gets a closer shave!

BRAVE MEN SHALL NOT DIE BECAUSE *I* FALTERED

Connie Matsuo recalls standing with her husband in a Winnipeg hall 46 years ago while farmers chose laborers like cattle from a group of Japanese Canadians who had just arrived from British Columbia. "We were just about the last ones picked because we had two old parents and I had just had a baby."

— From "Ottawa Apologizes to Internees," *Winnipeg Free Press*, 23 September 1988

WARTIME WORK AT INCO

We were young, only twenty or so when we started at INCO in February 1943. We worked in the crushing plant, the concentrator (the mill), the dry in the electrical or machine shops, a few of us in the smelter. Women weren't allowed underground in those days. I was in the crushing plant. It was a dusty, dirty job but an easy watch. Rock came in from the miners as large stones and was crushed to fine gravel. I was a swing worker so I did most jobs. The men who supervised us were older, fifty or fifty-five, too old for the war. They treated us well, like their daughters, waking us up if we fell asleep on night shift and showing us how to do things.

One of our first jobs was removing wood from the conveyer belt. One time I looked over at a co-worker. She was on the floor, her severed arm some distance away. She had put her arm in to straighten a piece of wood and her hand was caught under the conveyer. It was her right arm too. It was the only accident in three years though.

We got our pink slips in November 1945. Men were coming back from the war. It was a bad day. We had made good friends; it was like a family after three years. We used to have an annual banquet, get out of our overalls and dress up. I'm still in touch with one friend from my work days but many of the women had come from out West, Ukrainian and Polish Canadians, and we lost touch. My husband had been in the Canadian army and returned from overseas. Shortly after everything returned to "normal" and we returned home and raised families. That's what people did in those days.

— Vi Cepetelli, Copper Cliff, Ontario (as told to M. Bardswich)
Vi Cepetelli was one of the female employees at Inco during World War II.

JAPANESE INTERNMENT

Farmers of the Red River Valley and Adjacent Municipalities
DO YOU NEED FARM HELP?

The Dominion Government has made provision for removal of Japanese from British Columbia restricted areas. Thus farm labor reinforcements are now available to Manitoba farmers. The thorough agricultural knowledge of the Canadian Japanese cannot be stressed too highly and farmers taking advantage of this wartime move are enabled not only to assist in a problem arising out of national necessity duty in doing so are alleviating the farm labor shortage which is steadily increasing.

STUDY THESE ADVANTAGES
a. These Japanese are being drawn from thoroughly experienced agriculturists fully familiar with every type of farming.
b. The Canadian Japanese is both industrious and loyal, having spent his entire life in accordance with Canadian standards of living.
c. Japanese to be moved into Manitoba in furtherance of this scheme will be moved at the expense of the Commission who will assume full responsibility for the Japanese while they are in the district and will move them out of the district as soon as the emergency ceases to exist or they are required to be moved in the best interests of the district concerned.

Applications for employing of Japanese families with a full statement of ability to meet governing conditions should be made through the British Columbia Security Commission.

(Grain Exchange, Winnipeg 1942)

Above: Poster offering free Japanese labour. In 1942, all Japanese Canadians were placed in internment camps. Some men were sent to work camps to help build roads or railways. A large number ended up on sugar beet farms in the prairies. Many preferred the farms because families would not be broken up. However, living conditions were primitive and life was harsh.

(NAC C-49392)

ADJUSTING TO POST-WAR LIFE

Left: Veterans learning the building trades at the Edmonton Rehabilitation School. A new government Department of Veterans Affairs was created to help with rehabilitation and handle pensions. The Veterans Land Act would help returning service personnel set up farms, purchase fishing boats or build homes. The government also organized transportation for more than 40 000 war brides and over 20 000 children of overseas servicemen. Nevertheless it was often difficult for soldiers to adjust to civilian life and for war brides to adjust to life in a new country.

Right: Over 35 000 veterans take advantage of government education grants, enrolling in universities across the country. Veteran enrolment was greater than the total university enrolment prior to the war.

(NAC PA-116069)

WOMEN

In Peace As In War

PROTECT YOUR HOME

INFLATION

(NAC PA-93674)

Left: Chocolate Bar Boycott, Montreal, Quebec, 1947. Protests against rising prices were common in 1946. Prices seemed to rise as controls were eased but wages seemed to remain low. And, while workers had savings from wartime jobs, bonuses for overtime work and women's wages had generally dried up.

"With the gradual increase in production, the need for limitations on the expansion of purchasing power has decreased...it was only a matter of time before there would no longer be a need for wage and salary control in the battle against inflation."

— Prime Minister Mackenzie King announces the end of war-time wage and salary controls, 30 November 1946

"...married women who have become... stenographers and who were offered such positions as char women, assistants to laundries, ironers, work at slicing bread, icing cakes, baby sitting, housekeeping and so on. When they report that they are unwilling to take positions of this kind and feel that they should not be asked to take them within the meaning of the words 'suitable employment,' they are simply told by the people in the offices to whom they appeal that nothing can be done..."

— Stanley Knowles (CCF Party), House of Commons Debates, 14 July 1947

The experience of the past decade is conclusive evidence that unemployment relief should be a dominion function. By unemployment relief we mean relief or aid for unemployed employables as distinct from unemployables. Provincial responsibility for other welfare services should continue and the provinces should be enabled financially to perform these services adequately.

— *Rowell-Sirois Report*, 1940

During the war I felt like I was somebody, I was recognized, and then it was all over and I was nobody again. My family didn't seem to care what I'd done. I was just supposed to forget all that and fit in. It wasn't quite that simple.

— Former member, RCAF (WD), *Greatcoats and Glamour Boots, Canadian Women at War (1939-45)*

LABOUR ACTIONS

The Canadian Seamen's Union was a powerful communist-led union in the 1940s. In 1949, with the support of the Canadian government, management, and some labour leaders, the American Seafarers International Union took over the CSU. Over the next decade, there were wage increases and improved working conditions but also secret deals with shipping companies, violence, and blackmail. The CSU was suspended from the Canadian Labour Congress in 1959 and in 1963, following the report of a government commission, placed under trusteeship. The Seafarers International Union is still the main seamen's union in the country.

Below: Aurom Yanofsky paints a protest mural.
In February 1949, the four month long Asbestos Strike started illegally with 5 000 members of the Canadian Catholic Confederation of Labour and spread to other mines, many American owned. Premier Maurice Duplessis sent in large numbers of Quebec Provincial Police. The Church split with the government and supported the strikers. Intellectuals and activists such as Pierre Trudeau also supported the strikers, and the Asbestos Strike became a symbol of change in Quebec.

(NAC PA-124364)

FORD MOTOR COMPANY STRIKE

(Archives of Labour and Urban Affairs, Wayne State University)

6:00 A.M., 5 November 1945. Members of UAW Local 200 illegally blockade the Ford Plant at Windsor. It was almost two months into the strike when workers used this novel approach to prevent police from gaining access to the plant. Using vehicles to bar the way, thousands joined the picket line, singing and marching. The strike ended just before Christmas.

The Ford Motor Company's strike in September 1945 was "a classic battle for union security." The UAW wanted compulsory union membership with union dues automatically deducted from workers' salaries (i.e. payroll checkoff). The strike ended in arbitration where, in a landmark decision, Justice Rand ruled that while dues could be checked off to unions, workers should have the right to decide for themselves whether or not to join the union. A version of the Rand Formula has been negotiated by unions throughout Canada and in many provinces it has legal status.

GIVES DECISION

MR. JUSTICE I.C. RAND

Member of the Supreme Court of Canada and government appointed sole arbiter in the dispute between the labor union and the Ford Motor Co. of Canada, who yesterday handed down a decision in the case. His formula is designed to give both union and company security...

— University of New Brunswick

27

1950 - 1959

1951	1951	1952
Old Age Assistance Act & Old Age Security Act; Indian Act is amended	Canadian Psychiatric Association formed	United Textile Workers Strike

THE POSTWAR ECONOMIC BOOM lasted throughout the 1950s. Maintaining social stability and strengthening social welfare was a priority. Old Age Security and Unemployment Insurance were improved. Federal and provincial Fair Employment Practices acts were enacted.

Workers were unwilling to return to the dangerous working conditions and low paying jobs that had characterized many industries prior to the war. Union security gained from PC 1003, the Rand Formula, and the rapid growth in membership boosted labour's confidence. Women joined the workforce in increasing numbers. White-collar unions of nurses, civil servants, and teachers were organizing.

There were strikes in almost every province and every industry – loggers, fishers, government workers, autoworkers, gold miners, nickel miners and smelter workers and others walked off the job at some point during the 1950s. While most strikes were peaceful and advanced the interests of workers, some, like the Newfoundland loggers strike, ended in violence, death, and defeat for the union. However, growing confidence hid internal problems. At the same time that older craft unions and newer industrial unions were joining together to form the Canadian Labour Congress (CLC), Cold War politics were dividing the labour movement. Communist-led unions were expelled from the CLC, as were their supporters.

Government housing policy helped create planned suburban neighbourhoods and new towns to meet the needs of postwar society. The federal government also embarked on a program to improve housing for Natives on reserves and for Metis — one-room plywood shacks without insulation, running water, electricity, or indoor toilets were built.

The "baby boom" placed demands for educational opportunities. The booming economy needed workers with technical skills. The Diefenbaker government gave provinces money to build comprehensive technical high schools. In Quebec, university students demanded changes to Quebec's church-run education system. Natives wanted an end to residential schools. While more Natives were being educated in provincial schools, First Nations values and culture were still not being taught.

Canadian attitudes toward health care were also undergoing change. Health care was available to those who could afford it. Private health insurance was expensive and discriminated against those who suffered from mental illness. As CCF premier of Saskatchewan, Tommy Douglas campaigned for medicare to ensure that everyone would have equal and adequate access to doctors and hospitals. The first universal, government-run medicare system was established in Saskatchewan in 1962.

(Walter Curtin/NAC PA-137090)

The Canadian Congress of Labour merged with Trades and Labour Canada in June 1955 to form the Canadian Labour Congress (CLC). This ended the division between industrial and craft unions.

A physiotherapist works with 2 1/2 year-old Gifford at a polio clinic at the Sudbury General Hospital. A doll placed at the end of the bars encourages Gifford to walk. Although a vaccine was developed in 1954, many people suffered paralysis and longterm disability from polio.

"All things being equal, I'd say the brunette on the end just doesn't measure up..."

Above: Under the Female Employees Fair Remuneration Act of 1951, women in Ontario cannot be discriminated against financially because of their sex, with penalties of up to $100 for individuals and organizations found guilty of discrimination.

Top left: Poster protesting the use of public funds to create affordable housing.

Middle: The Honourable Ellen Fairclough was the first female cabinet minister. She was appointed Minister of Citizenship and Immigration on 21 June 1957. In the picture, a young refugee allowed into Canada in 1959 during World Refugee Year, gives Ms. Fairclough a kiss.

Right: James Gladstone (left) was appointed the first Native Senator on 1 February 1958. In this picture, he's shown with friends on the Blood Indian Reserve, Alberta.

SPRINGHILL MINE DISASTER

1950 – 1959

A starving Padleimiut woman consoles her child at camp on South Henik Lake near Padlei, Northwest Territories, February 1950.

"…if 14 people in any part of Canada other than that part which I have the honor to represent were to die of starvation the entire country would be aroused in indignation that conditions of this kind could exist in our society."

— M.A. Hardie, MP for Mackenzie River, in a House of Commons speech about the 14 Inuit who starved because of the depletion of caribou herds, and had to resort to eating their own clothes.

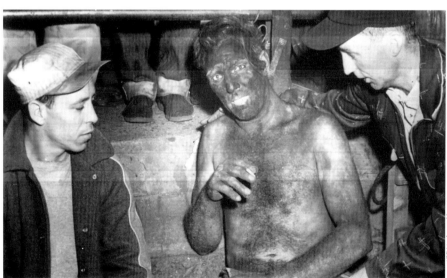

"They're all dead."

— unidentified miner after his rescue from Springhill Mine

Layton Amon, his body covered with coal dust, arrives at the pithead following his rescue from No. 2 mine at Springhill, N.S., on 24 October 1958.
On 23 October 1958, in one of the country's worst mine disasters, a "bump" occurred at No. 2 Cumberland mine, the deepest coal mine in North America. A "bump" is when stresses in a coal pillar, left for support in underground workings, cause the pillar to rupture without warning, sending coal and rock flying with explosive force. Many survivors of the shift of 167 men were brought to the surface with serious injuries, some after as long as a week underground. The 74 deaths were caused by dehydration and suffocation. The miners had been trapped in gas-filled pockets at coal faces at the 3990- and 3960-metre depths.

1960 - 1969

1960

Technical and Vocational Training Assistance Act allows Ottawa to join the provinces in funding capital costs for vocational training schools

1960

4 Aug: Canadian Bill of Rights approved by House of Commons

BOB DYLAN'S SONG "The times, they are a-changin'" captured the essence of the turbulent 1960s, a decade of youthful rebellion against the "establishment," of demonstrations for world peace, for justice and civil rights, for racial and sexual equality, for the eradication of poverty, for better education, and protests against American involvement in the Vietnam War. It was also the decade of "sex, drugs and rock'n'roll."

After their contributions to World War II, First Nations people felt that they had earned the right to be full participants in society. They agitated for and got the right to vote. They fought for the abolition of a system that denied Native status for women who married non-Native men but maintained it for men who married non-Native women.

University students staged sit-ins, "teach-ins" and other types of protest against the Vietnam War, the destruction of the environment, the way their universities were being governed, and many other issues. McGill University students marched for "McGill français," demanding French as the language of instruction, a reduced tuition fee, and public access to the McLennan Library. Black students destroyed the computers at Sir George Williams University in Montreal to protest discriminatory practices at the institution. Meanwhile, politicians in Halifax bulldozed "Africville," the city's black community, to "clean up the area."

A new wave of feminists demanded to be recognized as people in their own right – not as extensions of the men in their lives. They wanted equal pay for work of equal value, control over their own bodies, and the government out of their personal relationships. To achieve these goals, women's groups came together across the country. The 1968 Royal Commission on the Status of Women had a profound effect on the Feminist Movement. As Justice Minister, and later as Prime Minister, Pierre Trudeau legalized the distribution of birth control information and decriminalized abortion and homosexuality, stating "the state has no place in the bedrooms of the nation."

Demands for social change were being made everywhere. Royal Commissions, Senate committees, special task forces and legislative reforms were committed to improving the lives of the "have-nots." Following the lead of U.S. President Johnson, the federal government announced its own "war on poverty." Increasing urbanization brought concerns about communities and neighbourhoods, land use and development, efficient transportation networks, pollution, access to clean water and other resources to the forefront of municipal politics. Demands for adequate, affordable housing for the poor, led to some of the first social housing developments. The country definitely was "a-changin'."

THE TIMES THEY ARE A-CHANGIN'

Come mothers and fathers
Throughout the land
And don't criticize
What you can't understand
Your sons and your daughters
Are beyond your command
Your old road is
Rapidly agin'.
Please get out of the new one
If you can't lend your hand
For the times they are a-changin'.

(NAC PA-127290)

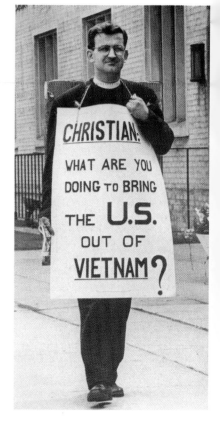

Above: Reverend Dan Heap pickets outside the Anglican Synod office, 1966.

Left: Therese Casgrain founded the Quebec chapter of Voices of Women in 1961.

UNIVERSAL SOLDIER*

He's 5 foot 2 and he's 6 feet 4
And he fights with missiles and with spears
He's all of 31 and he's only 17
And he's been a soldier for a thousand years

He's fighting for Democracy,
he's fighting for the Reds
He says it's for the peace of all
He's the one, who must decide,
who's to live and who's to die
And he never sees the writing on the walls

He's the universal soldier
And he really is the blame
But his orders comes from
far away no more

They come from him
And you and me
Oh, brothers can't you see
This is not the way we put an end to war

(photo courtesy of the Nihewan Foundation)

Buffy Sainte-Marie was born on a Cree reservation in Saskatchewan, Canada, and was a popular protest singer in the 1960s.

1961	1961	1962	1963
New Democratic Party formed to replace CCF	Prime Minister John Diefenbaker gives anti-apartheid speech which influences South Africa to withdraw from Commonwealth	1 July: Medicare in Saskatchewan; last execution takes place in Toronto	Front de Liberation du Quebec (FLQ) begins bombing campaign in Montreal

(York University/Neg#1740)

(York University)

Above left: Public opinion turned against the unions when the striking tannery workers took their dispute to the homes of other workers. Strikers took their children along to dispel the suspicion that the picketer was "watching and besetting" for intimidation purposes.

Above right: Hamilton police remove a worker during a violent wildcat strike at Stelco in 1966. The workers were angry with their unions and the company. The violence indicated a growing frustration in the new generation of workers.

MARY GOT A NEW JOB

Mary got a new job, workin' on the line
Help to make the automobile.
Wasn't very long 'til the job was going fine
And she liked the way it made her feel.
It gave her independence to drive into the lot
And pull her heavy work clothes on.
She liked the rush and clatter,
She liked her new friends
And her fav'rite was a man named John.

John was like a brother, workin' at her side
And they both came on the job the same day,
Learned the job together,
How the ropes were tied.
Went together down to draw their first pay.
Opening up his packet, Johnny dropped his cash
Money was all over the floor.
Mary saw the money, saw to her surprise
Johnny had a whole lot more, and she said:

Chorus:
"Who's been matching you
sweat for sweat?
Who's been working on the line,
Who's been earning what she ain't got yet?
All I want is what's mine.
I've got hands & eyes & a back like you
And I use them hard the whole day.
I stand here working just as hard as you do
And I want my equal pay."

— Tom Paxton

(Glenbow NA-1312-2)

Women in Edmonton protest their firing after demanding a "living wage" from their employer, the Edmonton Club.

1960 – 1969

31

Quebec-1963: Amendment to HOTELS ACT

8. No owner or keeper of a hotel, restaurant or camping ground shall directly or through his agent or a third party:

a. refuse to provide any person or class of persons with lodging, food or any other services offered to the public in the establishment, or

b. exercise any discrimination to the detriment of any person or class of persons as regards lodging, food or any other service offered to the public in the establishment, because of the race, belief, colour, nationality, ethnic origin or place of birth of such person or class of persons.

The Canadian Bill of Rights, 1960, was signed by Prime Minister John Diefenbaker (left). Although the Bill applied only to federal law since the consent of the provinces was not obtained, it was a pioneering step in safeguarding Canadians' civil liberties.

PART I: BILL OF RIGHTS

1. It is hereby recognized and declared that in Canada there have existed and shall continue to exist without discrimination by reason of race, national origin, colour, religion or sex, the following human rights and fundamental freedoms, namely,

(a) the right of the individual to life, liberty, security of the person and enjoyment of property, and the right not to be deprived thereof except by due process of law;

(b) the right of the individual to equality before the law and the protection of the law;

(c) freedom of religion;

(d) freedom of speech;

(e) freedom of assembly and association; and

(f) freedom of the press.

YOU ARE ON INDIAN LAND

According to the Mohawks, the Jay Treaty of 1794 exempted them from cross-border duties. The Supreme Court of Canada held that these basic Indian rights had been cancelled by the Migratory Birds Convention Act and Customs Act. In November 1968, when customs officers clamped down on them, the Indians blockaded the Seaway International Bridge and were jailed on charges of obstructing the police.

"Indians are different. We aren't like white people. We don't want to chase the dollars the way you do. We don't want to cut down all the trees for a profit. We want to be able to take off in the summer when it's nice out and take our kids and say, 'Look how beautiful this land is.' And go fishing. You don't do that until you have a lot of money. But it's too late then. You're old by then. When we do it you say we're lazy.

A lot of white people wonder why we want special status but they forget what we gave up. Our forefathers earned these rights and I want to make sure they aren't lost. I can work here or anywhere. For me that border isn't there. I want my kids to be able to work anywhere too, because they're Indians. But every year they take away a little more. The Seaway chopped up our lands. They came and took our lands and when we said, 'How much will we get?' they said, 'We'll work something out.' But they didn't take the white lands, oh no, that was too expensive. They would never take the white man's land when they could get ours – after all ours couldn't cost much, there was nothing on it but trees. But we like those trees.

They've polluted our air and our water. Our trees are rotting and the cows die and you say we were the savages. You still try to get us to give up our culture and our customs. Well I'm going to tell you – on Saturday night the longhouse is filled with the young ones and they are all dancing the dances of their people. We will not give up our Indian ways."

— Mike Mitchell, a former Grand Chief of the Mohawk Council of Akwesasne for the Akwesasne Reserve located near Cornwall, Ontario, "Personal Story of Mike Mitchell" *Weekend Magazine*, 19 April 1969

(CP/Halifax Chronicle Herald)

AFRICVILLE

For 150 years, descendants of American slaves who fled to Canada lived in Africville, a ghetto bordered by railway tracks and garbage and sewage disposal sites. The area was described in a Halifax, Nova Scotia, report of the 1950s as "a jumble of shacks, where 70 negro families live in deplorable conditions…these families must be moved out, and the land must be made available to the future city needs."

Africville was finally demolished and its residents relocated in 1969, with only a small compensation for their homes. The demolition of Africville and the Sir George William Computer riots were pivotal events highlighting the racism still to be found in Canada in the 1960s. It is still a challenge to obtain primary documents that tell these stories.

(CP/Blaise Edwards)

THE PILL

Few scientific inventions have changed society as much as the contraceptive pill. Since it went on the market in 1961, The Pill has been credited with launching the women's movement. Birth control wasn't legalized until 1969. Before that, Canadians still used contraceptives despite the law, buying them "under the counter" at drug stores. By 1966, over 750 000 women were using The Pill as their method of birth control.

Left: Prime Minister Pierre Trudeau dances with a supporter during an election campaign stop in Toronto, 19 June 1968. "Trudeaumania" swept the country and Trudeau led the Liberal Party to the first majority government since 1958.

"We believe in two official languages and in a pluralistic society, not nearly as a political necessity but as an enrichment."

— Pierre Trudeau, 17 October 1968, introducing the Official Languages Bill to Parliament

MEDICARE CRISIS 1962

Dr.F.N.ALCANTARA	Dr.W.CHEN	Dr.D.F.P.GORDON	Dr.J.P.KIM	Dr.D.
Dr.W.S.ALLAN	Dr.C.J.CHOUINARD	Dr.F.J.A.GORMAN		Dr.J.I.
Dr.J.P.ALPORT	Dr.T.A.CHRISTIE	Dr.G.S.GR	LAIDLAW	Dr.E.C.
Dr.W.E.H.ALPORT	Dr.S.COHEN	Dr.H.C.GR	ARSEN	Dr.D.M
Dr.J.D.ANDERSON	Dr.C.L.COMRIE		AWBY	Dr.F.H
Dr.J.C.ARMIT	Dr.L.E.COWAN	Dr.F.A.HA	AXDAL	Dr.J.I
Dr.E.ASQUITH	Dr.R.A.CROOK	Dr.D.C.H	WCRAFT	Dr.E.L
Dr.A.BABCHUK	Dr.C.H.CROSBY	Dr.T.J.HA	AZARUS	
Dr.B.BACHYNSKI	Dr.C.L.CUNNING	Dr.M.HEIMBA	LeBLOND	
Dr.E.W.BARDOTES	Dr.N.M.CUTLER	Dr.H.A.HENGE	LDUS	
Dr.M.P.BARRY		Dr.N.L.G.HOFFMAN	OUT	
Dr.I.W.BEAN	Dr.W.A.OAKIN	Dr.R.T.HOSIE		Dr.L.N
Dr.E.P.BENSON	Dr.J.H.DANBY	Dr.M.HUBAR		M.D.
Dr.S.C.BEST	Dr.N.E.J.DAVIES	Dr.A.HUDE		
Dr.T.M.BLACK	Dr.R.A.L.DAVIS	Dr.A.F.		
Dr.L.S.BOWER	Dr.H.B.S.DeGROOT			
Dr.M.W.BOWERING	Dr.F.C.DOBIE	Dr.M		
Dr.T.A.B.BOYD	Dr.B.P.DUNCAN	Dr.F		
Dr.G.C.BRADLEY	Dr.E.H.DUNCAN	Dr.H		
Dr.J.A.BROWN	Dr.G.E.ELLIOTT			
Dr.J.L.BROWN				
Dr.T.E.BUGG	Dr.K.H.FICKE			
	Dr.M.FINKELSTEIN			
Dr.J.A.CARMICHAEL	Dr.M.M.FRASER			
Dr.D.W.CARNDUFF				
Dr.T.CARTMILL	Dr.U.J.GAREAU			
Dr.L.A.CAWSEY	Dr.H.C.GEORGE			

(CP/Regina Leader-Post)

Doctors' Strike: Every single doctor is registered as "OUT" at the Regina General Hospital, 2 July 1962.

(NAC C-36222)

Tommy Douglas at the founding convention of the New Democratic Party, August 1961.

"…Mr. Speaker,…To me it seems to be sheer nonsense to suggest that medical care is something which ought to be measured just in dollars. When we're talking about medical care we're talking about our sense of values. Do we think human life is important? Do we think that the best medical care which is available is something to which people are entitled, by virtue of belonging to a civilized community?"

— Tommy Douglas, speech, *The Case for Universal Health Insurance*, 1961

1960
–
1969

1970 - 1979

1970	1970	1970
Royal Commission on the Status of Women presents its report	Oct: FLQ Crisis – Quebec Labour Minister kidnapped and strangled	Nova Scotian Winston Ruc becomes first black presiden United Steel Workers of Ame

THE 1970s WAS A DECADE of radical politics, increased labour militancy, second wave feminism, and intensified anti-war protests. Environmental awareness and aboriginal activism increased. The Urban Alliance on Race Relations was founded, and the Multicultural Act and Canadian Human Rights Act were passed.

Better educated than their parents, the first of the baby boomers began to enter the job market, demanding improved salaries and benefit packages to keep up with both inflation and rising expectations of a better life. Groups not traditionally militant took to the picket line. Teachers, nurses, hospital workers, even police and firefighters went on strike. To fight inflation, the Trudeau government imposed wage controls in 1975.

Women's issues focused on pay equity, equal rights in the workplace, and the right to abortion. The 1970 federal Report on the Status of Women emphasized the freedom of women to choose whether to work outside the home or not, shared parental responsibility for child care, and anti-discrimination in the workplace. The National Action Committee on the Status of Women (NAC) was formed to prod the government to enact the Report's recommendations and to raise awareness of women's issues. Changes did occur. The principle of "equal pay for work of equal value" was established for federal government employees and in most provinces, and in 1977 the Canadian Human Rights Act outlawed discrimination, including gender bias.

Across Canada many working people associated economic problems with American control of Canadian businesses and were concerned about Canadian labour's ties with U.S. unions. The Committee for an Independent Canada was formed. During the minority government of 1972-74, the New Democratic Party forced Trudeau to adopt a more nationalist stance and create the Foreign Investment Review Agency to monitor American purchases of Canadian companies.

A major concern was our shared environment with the U.S. The Great Lakes Quality Agreement would lead to initiatives to ban phosphate emissions and to clean up the lakes, especially Lake Erie. The newly formed Pollution Probe, targeted phosphate emissions as well as the use of DDT and encouraged municipal recycling.

Aboriginal Canadians became politically active to protect their traditional way of life and the environment. The Mackenzie Valley Pipeline Inquiry stopped that project to assess the environmental impact and begin to settle the land claims of the Dene. In 1975, the landmark James Bay Agreement was signed between the Cree and the Quebec government before Hydro Quebec could begin work on the Great Whale hydro project.

(WAHC)

The Feminist Revolution continued in Quebec as in the rest of Canada. Women began to consider careers in male dominated professions such as medicine, business, engineering, and law. There was a call for "equal pay for work of equal value." Social activists concentrated on poverty issues, calling for improved day care, affordable housing, and better welfare. The National Action Committee on the Status of Women was started in 1970 as an umbrella organization for 30 women's groups representing unions, aboriginal women, students, poverty activists, and women's shelters, among others.

(NAC PA-18687l)

"I am convinced that until we have more women in politics – openly, flagrantly and unashamedly committed to the struggle for the liberation of women and determined to change traditional power politics to make it more responsive to the dispossessed of this earth – we as women are doomed to many more years of oppression and exploitation."

— Rosemary Brown, 1977, social activist, first black female elected to the B.C. Legislature in 1972, serving as MLA for 14 years

"Through the centuries this relationship (between the sexes) has been a continuing power struggle in which women have been idolized, patronized, and exploited. Society's most arbitrary folly has been and continues to be its under-utilization of women's brain power. It is now time for women to be humanized, their brain power tapped, and their abilities recognized.

Women comprise the largest alienated element in our society. Yet it has taken two thousand years for women to move from passivity, to alienation, to their present anger...."

— Laura Sabia, activist for women's rights, founding member and first president of the National Action Committee on the Status of Women, 1978

THE URBAN ALLIANCE ON RACE RELATIONS

The Urban Alliance on Race Relations is an organization whose primary goal is to "promote a stable and healthy multi-racial environment in the community." The Alliance was founded by Dr. Wilson Head (1914–1993).

In the early 1970s, after Victoria's mayor suggested that long-haired hippies be prevented from disembarking from B.C. Ferries, a group of citizens formed Cool-Aid to provide shelter for young travellers. Funded by the federal government the group provided emergency housing, free meals, and a medical clinic for thousands of young people who had dropped out of mainstream society.

Above: Greenpeace began in Vancouver with a protest against American nuclear testing off the coast of Alaska and later took up other causes, opposing, for example, clear cut logging and indiscriminate killing of wildlife.

Below: 12 June 1970 – Demonstrators protest the arrest of Dr. Henry Morgentaler who openly set up abortion clinics in Montreal and Toronto to perform abortions despite the law which stipulated that they could only take place in hospitals with the approval of a committee of three doctors. Morgentaler was initially found not guilty, then guilty on appeal, and, during a third trial, not guilty. Morgentaler's arrests and trials focused attention on the abortion issue across Canada.

RELUCTANT HOSTS

...There is no need to catalogue here the extensive patterns of social, economic and political discrimination which developed against non-Anglo-Saxons...

Discrimination was one of the main factors which led to the transference (with only a few exceptions) of the same ethnic "pecking order" which existed in Immigration policy to the place each group occupied on the "vertical mosaic," with the British (especially the Scots) on top, and so on down to the Chinese and blacks who occupied the most menial jobs. Non-British and non-French groups not only had very little economic power; they also would not even significantly occupy the middle echelons of politics, education or the civil service until after World War II.

The ethnic stereotypes which developed for eastern European and Oriental groups emphasized their peasant origins. These stereotypes played a role in determining the job opportunities for new immigrants and functioned to disparage those who would climb out of their place...Names such as "Wops," "Bohunks" and especially "foreigner" indicated class as well as ethnic origin and these terms were used as weapons in the struggle for status...

— Howard Palmer, "Reluctant Hosts: Anglo-Canadian Views of Multiculturalism in the Twentieth Century," in *Multiculturalism as State Policy: Report of the Second Conference on Multiculturalism*

1970
–
1979

35

(RWDSU/Bill Hanes)

Above left: During a strike, women at Hanes Hosiery in Toronto "dress" to attract public attention. In the end they lost their fight for a union and many lost their jobs.

Above right: In July 1974, trawlermen in eight Newfoundland ports went on strike over their right to be considered "employees." Negotiation of income was to be based on time at sea rather than the number of fish caught. The strike finally ended in March with wage increase lower than those recommended by the mediator, but the trawlermen won the right to be considered "employees."

TEACHERS' STRIKES

Right: After a series of strikes in 1974 and 1975, teachers gained large salary increases and new benefits. By 1976 they were hit by the Anti-Inflation Board.

(Spectator/Hamilton Public Library, Special Image Coll.)

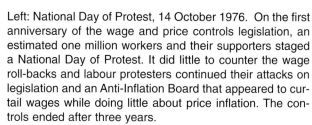

Left: National Day of Protest, 14 October 1976. On the first anniversary of the wage and price controls legislation, an estimated one million workers and their supporters staged a National Day of Protest. It did little to counter the wage roll-backs and labour protesters continued their attacks on legislation and an Anti-Inflation Board that appeared to curtail wages while doing little about price inflation. The controls ended after three years.

"The government's economic policies have caused hardship, economic suffering, and a loss of democratic bargaining rights...the government has refused to listen to any worker representatives who have tried to suggest positive ways of controlling inflation without hurting working people."

— Grace Hartman, National President Canadian Union of Public Employees, 1976

36

Highly skilled crew work on the Observation Lookout Point of the CN Tower in 1976.

The FLQ

"The Front de Liberation du Quebec is not a messiah, nor a modern-day Robin Hood. It is a group of Quebec workers who have decided to use all means to make sure that the people of Quebec take control of their own destiny....

We have had our fill of promises of jobs and prosperity while we always remain the cowering servants and boot lickers of the big shots...Production workers, miners, foresters, teachers, students and unemployed workers, take what belongs to you, your jobs, your determination and your liberty....Make your own revolution in your areas, in your places of work...

We are the workers of Quebec and we will go to the end...."

— Excerpt from the FLQ Manifesto of October 1970. It is a call for a workers' revolution as well as a call for a free Quebec.

The government believes as well that youth is sincere in its efforts to improve society and that young people are anxious to work and to engage in activities which are intended to make Canada a better place in which to live...The Opportunities for Youth program will combine the resources of the government with the resources of youth. We are saying, in effect, to the youth of Canada that we are impressed by their desire to fight pollution; that we believe they are well motivated in their concern for the disadvantaged; that we have confidence in their value system.

— Prime Minister Trudeau, House of Commons, 16 March 1971
Opportunities for Youth, a summer program for students, set up projects across the country and provided for almost 95 000 students.

CANADA'S TOP TEN UNIONS: 1979

		Members
1.	Canadian Union of Public Employees	250 000
2.	National Union of Provincial Government Employees	198 000
3.	United Steelworkers of America	195 000
4.	Public Service Alliance of Canada	160 000
5.	United Auto Workers	135 000
6.	United Food & Commercial Workers	115 000
7.	International Brotherhood of Teamsters	93 000
8.	United Brotherhood of Carpenters & Jointers	86 000
9.	Quebec Teachers Central	75 000
10.	Social Affairs Federation (Quebec)	72 000

WORK AT INCO

(The Inco Triangle Vol. 34 #8/August 1974)

Left to right: Laurene Wiens, Rachel Barriault and Melody Midena proudly check their cheques. All three are on the job at the Copper Cliff nickel refinery. They were the first of the feminine influx at Inco's Sudbury area operations.

1974....In the U.S. the World Trade Center opens and Barbara Walters becomes the first female news anchor. Golda Meir resigns as Prime Minister of Israel. And in Sudbury, Ontario, Inco Metals Company, the western world's largest producer of nickel prepares to hire women to work in its plants for the first time since World War II.

I was one of those women and I was lucky enough to be employed in the Copper Cliff Mill. I say "lucky" because the women who had worked there during the war had paved the way for us.

Not all the male employees were happy to see us there, however, and some were quite vocal about it. They questioned why we were not home having babies; others said we were taking jobs away from men; still others thought we were too frail to do the work.

Although the work is hard at times and shift-work interferes with family life, it has provided a good life for myself and my son. As a single mom, I have been able to buy a house, return to university, ensure my son's education, and travel.

Because we are members of Local 6500 of the United Steelworkers of America, our employment with Inco provides us with good salaries, benefits and pensions. The women who worked here during the Second World War would be impressed!

— Elizabeth Bardswich, 2002

1970 – 1979

1980 - 1989

1980	1982	1982	1982
Quebec referendum: "Non;" National Advisory Council on Aging formed	17 Apr: The Constitution Act signed	Severe recession begins	Beginning of "Decade of Disabl[e] Persons"

THE 1980s OPENED with a brief boom that was followed by the most serious economic downturn since the 1930s. By 1982, unemployment was higher in Canada than in any other developed country. Interest rates on loans rose to 21% and many could not pay their mortgages.

Unemployment Insurance benefits were cut and funds were used for job creation projects. At the same time, the Supreme Court liberalized the scope of unemployment insurance to include women on maternity and parental leave and workers on short term disability.

Section 15 of the Charter of Rights and Freedoms broadened the scope for court challenges by allowing new interpretations of old legislation. As protection of human rights gained new priority, the abortion law was struck down, discrimination on the basis of sexual orientation was challenged and disallowed, accused offenders were guaranteed rights, the mentally disabled were protected, and human rights considerations were prominent in land treaty negotiations between the government and First Nations.

The spirit of Canadian economic nationalism that swept the 1970s was declining in the face of the recession and the growing strength of globalization. The Canadian Auto Workers was formed after splitting from its American organization, the UAW. Bob White and Buzz Hargrove wanted to establish "made in Canada" labour solutions. By the end of the decade, Canadians were debating the Free Trade Agreement with the United States.

AIDS had become the new "plague" of the 20th century and challenged the "free love" and casual attitudes towards sex of the 1960s and '70s. National and international campaigns were mounted to develop awareness of this new, deadly menace.

In this decade, women leaders gained ground in many areas: Bertha Wilson became the first Supreme Court Justice in 1982, Jeanne Sauvé the first female Governor General in 1984, and Shirley Carr the first female president of the Canadian Labour Congress in 1986. However, the average woman's wage was still below that of the average man, and women were still subject to deadly violence at the hands of husbands, lovers and even strangers. The decade ended on a violent note when, on 6 December 1989, 14 female engineering students were murdered at the École Polytechnique in Montreal by a man who blamed feminists for all his problems.

CAN YOU GET AIDS from a TOILET SEAT?

I HAVE AIDS - PLEASE HUG ME, I CAN'T MAKE YOU SICK

SILENCE = DEATH

Medical studies show that AIDS virus cannot be transmitted by the following routes:

cups & glasses	cutlery
toilet seats	swimming pools
door handles	
mosquitoes and flying insects	

"**I have this vision. I want to take AIDS back into society, like any other disease. It will take a lot of time, education and effort, but most of all, we've got to eliminate the stigma of AIDS.**"

— Dr. Norbert Gilmore, Royal Victoria Hospital Immunologist and a leading Canadian authority on HIV/AIDS

In the **Canada Health Act of 1984**, Health Minister Monique Begin, described as "the mother of modern medicare," reaffirmed the five principles of medicare: universality, accessibility, comprehensiveness, portability, and public administration. The bill also disallowed extra billing by doctors. It gave Ottawa the power to deduct a matching amount from health transfers for every dollar a province allowed in extra-billing.

Josiah Henson 1789-1883   Canada 32   postage/postes

JOSIAH HENSON

Josiah Henson (1789-1883) was featured on this stamp issued by Canada Post in 1983 to celebrate his life as a community leader and "conductor" on the "Underground Railroad." Josiah Henson arrived in Canada on 28 October 1830 after escaping from slavery in Maryland. Once in Canada, he worked as a farm labourer and acted as a leader for other escaped slaves. He established the Dawn Settlement near what is now Chatham, Ontario, to provide blacks with a general education and a community. Josiah Henson is believed to be the inspiration for Harriet Beecher Stowe's *Uncle Tom's Cabin*. Tony Kew, a Toronto artist, has based this stamp design on an authentic portrait of Josiah Henson, combined with a symbolic rendering of the "Underground Railroad," which transported thousands of slaves to freedom.

(Canada Post Corporation/Designed by Tony Kew/1983)

Section 15 of the
Charter of Rights and Freedoms:

15 (1) Every individual is equal before and under the law and has the right to the equal protection and equal benefit of the law without discrimination and, in particular, without discrimination based on race, national or ethnic origin, colour, religion, sex, age or mental or physical disability.

15 (2) Subsection (1) does not preclude any law, program or activity that has as its object the amelioration of conditions of disadvantaged individuals or groups including those that are disadvantaged because of race, national or ethnic origin, colour, religion, sex, age or mental or physical disability.

(CP/Fred Chartrand)

Three years after Bertha Wilson's appointment as Supreme Court Justice, Section 15 of the Charter of Rights and Freedoms came into effect. It guaranteed the right to be free from discrimination. Bertha Wilson made the claim that there was now a "new role of judges, a fundamental reordering of the political balance of power." In Wilson's 10 years as a Supreme Court judge, Canadians saw more "liberal" interpretations of laws affecting the equality of individuals.

"There was a commitment that if we were unable to reach an agreement with Canada and the provinces dealing with constitutional protection [through the First Ministers Conferences] then they would do it in treaty agreements."

— Judy Gingell, former Council of Yukon Indians Chairperson and first Lieutenant Governor General of the Yukon

(CP)

In 1980, Terry Fox, who had lost a leg to cancer, began his Marathon of Hope, a run across Canada, to raise money for cancer research. Although the run ended midway when his cancer flared up again, millions of dollars were raised before his death the following year. Over $300 million has been raised in annual Terry Fox Runs around the world since then.

"Dreams are made if people only try.
I believe in miracles…I have to because somewhere the hurting must stop."
— Terry Fox

(CP)

Above: Citizen activists protest the testing of U.S. cruise missiles in Alberta, July 1983. Testing of BOMARC missiles in the 1960s had led to similar protests in the 1960s.

GAY COUPLES CAN BE A 'FAMILY'

13 April 1989: The tribunal of the Canadian Rights Commission rules that homosexual couples can constitute a family. New Democrat Sven Robinson calls it "an enlightened decision."

Free Trade Agreement

Right: Brian Mulroney signed the Free Trade Agreement with the U.S. The Agreement removed all protective trade tariffs between the two countries. Trade unions feared a loss of jobs to low-wage southern U.S. and Mexico. It remains a major issue among trade unionists today.

(NAC PA-164231)

"Mr. Speaker, Canadians have the fundamental ability to compete and excel. As a government, our responsibility is to provide the best environment possible to allow Canadians, individual Canadians, with their chance to succeed. I believe, Mr. Speaker, we can do this by endorsing the Free Trade Agreement today. By doing so, we say yes to free trade, yes to jobs for our youth, yes to a more prosperous future for Canada."

— Prime Minister Brian Mulroney, House of Commons, 1988

1980 — 1989

1990
International
Year of Literacy

1991
First Nations traditional
oath made in court instead
of swearing on Bible

1991
Canadians vote "No" to
Charlottetown Agreement

THE 1990S BEGAN with attempts to bring Quebec into the constitution. The Meech Lake Accord failed when Elijah Harper, a First Nations, NDP, MLA, prevented Manitoba from ratifying the agreement. "Distinct society" status could not belong to Quebec alone. After that, debate about First Nations' place in Canadian society grew until it reached a peak during the Oka crisis in 1990. First Nations leaders like Phil Fontaine, Ovide Mercredi and Judy Gingell worked with organizations like the Assembly of First Nations to develop agreements that would establish guidelines for solving land claims, treaty issues, hunting, logging, and fishing rights, and Native self-government.

Constitutional challenges forced institutions to recognize the growing diversity of Canadians. Sikh RCMP officers won the right to wear turbans in uniform and Black History Month became part of many school curriculums. School heritage language programs expanded, and school dress codes were required to accept religious dress, some even allowing the carrying of kirpans by Sikh students.

Fighting the deficit became the new political goal adopted by all provincial and federal governments which began cutting health and education spending. Health care and government workers staged "job actions" to voice their opposition. Education workers soon followed suit.

Government agencies, non-governmental agencies (NGOs), and individuals began assuming social responsibility for the world community. The Canadian International Development Agency (CIDA) led Canadian participation in programs to eradicate poverty, hunger, and illiteracy in many parts of the world. The NGO, *Medecins Sans Frontieres*/Doctors Without Borders, received the Nobel Peace Prize in 1999 for its work in war-torn nations. Young people such as Craig and Marc Kielburger founded "Kids Can Free the Children" and "Leaders of Today" to end child labour in the world. Canada was an active participant in world summits in Kyoto and Rio de Janeiro on global warming, renewable energy sources, and biodiversity, and in Cairo and Beijing on women's issues. Young people took to the streets in anti-globalization protests much as their parents had done to protest such things as the Vietnam War.

As the 20th century ended, many of the same problems that confronted Canadians at the beginning of the century were again on the rise. Tuberculosis, which had all but disappeared during the mid-century, was discovered among Natives and homeless people. Homelessness was declared a national disaster. Conditions for Natives on reserves remained substandard. First Nations land claims were unsettled. Canadians were trying to find solutions to dying fisheries, drought, air pollution, and contaminated water supplies.

We do not simply recognize and tolerate this diversity, but respect, value and nurture it as an exciting and integral part of our collective experience and identity.

— *Report on Diversity in Toronto*, 1990s

Hundreds of thousands of spectators turn up each year for the annual Gay Pride Parade in Toronto.

In 1988, Baltej Singh Dhillon, a Sikh immigrant, was accepted by the RCMP. When he was told that he could not wear his turban in uniform, he requested an exception be made, as the turban is a religious requirement of Sikhs. Over 200 000 Canadians signed a petition opposing it. Despite death threats, Dhillon stayed his course and in 1990, he won the legal right to wear the turban.

"We will stand on guard to make Canada a better place."
— RCMP Constable Baltej Singh Dhillon

"Let this decision be a wake up call for the Reform Party. Its opposition to Sikhs in the RCMP is out of line with the Canadian legal tradition and demonstrates an intolerance to cultural diversity. When will the Reform Party realize the 1930s are over? It is 1995 and the time has come for it to support the religious freedom of all Canadians."

— Harbance Singh Dhaliwal (Liberal MP Vancouver South) House of Commons, 1995

1992	1992	1993	1995
Corrections and Conditions Release Act replaces Penitentiary Act and Parole Act	Canada first country to sign International Biodiversity Agreement at Earth Summit meeting	North America Free Trade Agreement (NAFTA) signed	Royal assent given to self-government agreements between government and Yukon First Nations

Above: In January 1998, Federal Indian Affairs Minister Jane Stewart apologized on behalf of the Canadian Government to Phil Fontaine, National Chief of the Assembly of First Nations, for the mistreatment of aboriginal children in residential schools. Fontaine, himself a victim of physical and sexual abuse at a Catholic run residential school, received the apology and a $350-million 'healing fund.'

Right: On 16 July 1998, the federal and provincial governments signed a treaty with the Nisga'a nation giving 5 500 Nisga'a sovereignty over 200 000 hectares of land and a cash payment of $200 million. Supporters praised the treaty as a step toward First Nations' self-reliance and independence, but opponents criticized the government for "giving away the farm."

Above: Clifton Ruggles was a respected educator, artist, writer, and community activist, born and raised in Montreal. This painting, entitled *Invisibility Blues* reflects the everyday experiences and activities of the many members of Canada's complex Black society. This painting was also the cover of *Outsider Blues: A Voice from the Shadows*, a book co-authored with his wife, Olivia Rovinescu. The Quebec government distributed the image as the official Black History Month poster in 1999.

GREAT LAKES GETTING CLEANER?

Between 1991-1996, 10 tonnes of PCBs evaporated from Lakes

- bans on some chemicals mean fewer toxics are getting into Lakes – chemicals now leaving waters faster than they are replaced

- other chemicals leaving Lakes even faster – waters lost 11 times as much of pesticide dieldrin as they gained, a loss of 4 tonnes

- chemicals are carried about 200 kilometres at a time, a process known as the "grasshopper effect," before they fall out of atmosphere – long-lasting chemicals exhaled by Great Lakes will continue north until Arctic cold weather traps them

- estimated it will take 30 to 50 years for the lakes to cleanse themselves if atmosphere deposition of air pollutants is ended

1990 – 1999

41

EDUCATION

Teacher S. Fryer and her students at an Ontario high school represent the changing ethnic composition of Canada's classrooms.

MAKING CONTACT

Annual number of teaching days

Alberta	200
Manitoba	200
Quebec	200
Saskatchewan	197
Prince Edward Island	196
Canada	**195**
New Brunswick	195
Nova Scotia	195
British Columbia	194
Ontario	188
Newfoundland	185

THE COST OF LEARNING

Average spending per student, 1996-1997

Quebec	$7,032
British Columbia	6,882
Ontario	6,649
Manitoba	6,620
Canada	6,603
New Brunswick	6,156
Alberta	5,848
Saskatchewan	5,637
Nova Scotia	5,366
Prince Edward Island	5,148
Newfoundland	5,108

(Maclean's, 10 November 1997)

People who have not graduated from high school tend to be out of work longer. In the 1970s, people were unemployed for about the same length of time, no matter what their education. About six per cent of Canadians were looking for work. Today, with unemployment statistics around nine per cent - and nearly double that figure for youth - people with fewer than nine years of schooling are out of work five to seven weeks longer than people with more education. There are fewer jobs for people without a high school diploma.

— Council of Ministers of Education, *Report on Education in Canada 1998*

HEALTH

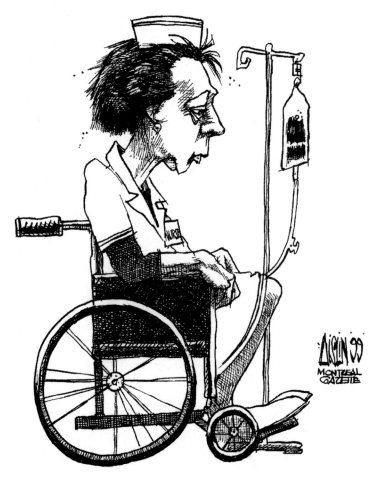

Nurses object to working conditions throughout Canada.

"Women who become pregnant through rape or incest should not qualify for government-funded abortions unless their pregnancy is life-threatening, says Labor Minister **Stockwell Day**"
Edmonton Journal, June 9, 1995

(CP/Kevin Frayer)

Canada's foremost abortion rights advocate Dr. Henry Morgentaler stands next to a sign quoting Canadian Alliance leader Stockwell Day during a news conference in Toronto, 21 November 2000. Morgentaler urged people to vote against what he called the Canadian Alliance's "hidden anti-choice agenda."

"In Canada, on average, 10 persons were infected with HIV every single day."

— Health Minister Allan Rock, Dec. 1998

The UN estimates that, as of 1998, almost 33.5 million people worldwide were infected with HIV. 43% of that number were women.

1997
Ontario teachers walk out against Harris government changes to curriculum and budget cuts

1998
West-coast Aboriginals continue to log despite government regulations; Aboriginal and non-Aboriginal disputes over fishing rights on east coast

1999
1 Apr: Nunavut created

1999
7 Oct: Adrienne Clarkson becomes Governor General

Crackdown heats up against squeegee kids

Harris, Lastman, Boothby want them off streets

The squeegee wars have begun.

The most telling sign is a crackdown by Toronto police…which led to arrests of at least 30 squeegee kids this past week.

Then the head of the province's Crime Control Commission Task Force, on instructions from Premier Mike Harris, said he was looking for a way to force them off the street.

Add to that comments by Police Chief David Boothby, who said if the province outlawed the practice under the Highway Traffic Act he could rid Toronto of every squeegee kid in Toronto within two weeks, and by Mayor Mel Lastman, who vowed to get the "thugs" off the streets, and it sounds like a full-scale assault.

"We are going to get them off the streets," Lastman vowed… "Many of them are thugs…All they're doing is intimidating people into giving them money. They're beggars, and that's all they are…The police are going to do everything they have to to get them off the streets."

— Phinjo Gombu, *Toronto Star,* 23 July 1998

ANTI-GLOBALIZATION

Above: A demonstrator is helped after getting pepper spray in her eyes. Police used pepper spray to break up a demonstration outside the University of British Columbia, the site of the APEC Summit in Vancouver, 25 November 1997. Several demonstrators were arrested when they tried to pull down a security fence.

"These kamikaze capitalists are not too far from the evil-doers…We are indeed surrounded by fundamentalists, religious and economic….We all need to rethink our attitude towards turbo-capitalism; it is a cry for help. We need to save these people!"

— Naomi Klein, anti-globalization activist and author

Above: In the 1980s the Mulroney government cut funding to social programs in order to reduce the deficit. By 1992 an estimated two million Canadians had turned to food banks across the country for their meals.

	Canada[1]	United States[2]
1991		
Number of strikes and lockouts	463	40
Workers involved (thousands)	253.4	392.0
Workdays not worked (thousands)	2516.0	4583.6
1997		
Number of strikes and lockouts	279	29
Workers involved (thousands)	253.6	338.6
Workdays not worked (thousands)	3568.8	4497.1

[1] Excluding work stoppages involving less than 10 workdays.
[2] Excluding work stoppages involving less than 1000 workers and lasting less than a full day or shift.

(International Labour Office/Yearbook of Labour Statistics, Geneva 1998)

1990
–
1999

Into the 21st Century

EDUCATION

The New Knowledge Citizen/Consumer is King:
The marriage of the most highly educated generation in our history and the…Internet places phenomenal power in the hands of a newly enfranchised class of knowledge citizens and consumers.

— *Searching for Certainty,* D. Bricker and E. Greenspon, 2001

INTERNET ACCESS, 2000

THE DIGITAL DIVIDE is often used to describe the uneven pattern between Internet access and usage

Aged 18 - 34	85%
Aged 55 and over	45%
Higher income group	88%
Lower income group	52%
University educated	85%
Non-university	46%

Households with Internet Connection
1995 – **10%**   1997 – **25%**   2000 – **over 50%**

URBAN REFORM

(Rick Eglinton/Toronto Star)

Redefining the Ghetto

"We might not have the clothes that rich people do, or the cars and houses, but we have what we need – food, friends, good teachers."

— Michell Atkinson, a Grade 8 student at Nelson Mandela Park Public School in Toronto

Students…are challenging perceptions of their community. Sure, there are problems where they live. But the kids point out that it's a neighbourhood and it's their home – not a stereotype.

— *The Toronto Star*, 18 May 2002

(Graeme MacKay)

Standardized Testing: In 2002, Ontario students joined students from other provinces in writing compulsory provincial literacy tests.

GLOBALIZATION: What's the alternative?

Fair – not free – trade
This means that people – not corporations, the International Monetary Fund, or the World Bank – make the decisions. It means trade and international deals that protect national sovereignty and the environment, and reduce social and economic inequalities. It means using trade and investment to achieve development, not just for profits.

— Canadian Labour Congress

(CP/Paul Chiasson)

Above: G8 Summit – a group of protesters dressed as soccer-playing G8 country leaders, are given a red card by an African referee during an early-morning demonstration in Calgary, 27 June 2002. The G8 leaders were to be discussing African aid and investment at the Kananaskis retreat.

LABOUR

'I serve but am silent' was the motto of the traditional nurse. But after two decades of growing activism, Canadian nurses have found their voice.

There has been a nursing strike or the threat of job action in almost every Canadian province in the past four years. 85% of Canadian nurses are unionized, compared to 10% of their counterparts in the United States. They are also politically active, taking positions on everything from free trade to social housing. The National Post looks at the political awakening of Canada's nursing profession.

— "Silent No More," *National Post*, 18 May 2002

Angry health care workers protest in Halifax on 27 June 2001. Premier John Hamm's government passed Bill 68 that removed the right to strike from health care workers.

HIV AIDS

Global Estimates End-2000
Children and Adults

People living with HIV/AIDS	36.1 million
New HIV infections in 2000	5.3 million
Deaths due to HIV/AIDS in 2000	3.0 million
Cumulative No. of deaths due to HIV/AIDS	21.8 million

℞ **8,000 PEOPLE WILL DIE OF AIDS TODAY BECAUSE TREATING THEM IS NOT "COST - EFFECTIVE"**

I prescribe that the canadian Government take immediate steps to fight the AIDS pandemic:

- commit funds and support clear treatment policies

Human Rights Activist Honoured

In May 2002, York University presented 94-year-old Lee Williams with an honorary Doctor of Laws degree. A former local chairman of the Order of Sleeping Car Porters' Union, Mr. Williams spent his first 30 years with CNR fighting discrimination from both his employer and union. Black employees were limited to sleeping car porters and paid "starvation wages." In 1964, the federal government ordered CNR to end discrimination, and black workers won the right to work as conductors and supervisors, which Mr. Williams ultimately did.

(Ruth Bonneville)

HEALTH CARE ISSUES

The siren wails. Once again, the Emergency ward is overflowing. The call resounds throughout Toronto East General: 'We need beds!'

Code Zero

— *The Saturday Star*, 25 May 2002

PM says we will pay to sustain medicare, doing it...

'The Canadian Way'

— *The Toronto Star*, 2 October 2002

In September 2000 the Federal government injected $21.5 billion into health care funds and 64% of Canadians named health care as their top concern.

— *Searching for Certainty*, D. Bricker and E. Greenspon, 2001

DISCRIMINATION

Support Levels for Gays in Different Occupations

	1988	2001
Salesperson	72%	93%
Armed Forces	60%	82%
Doctor	52%	82%
Prison Officer	44%	75%
Junior School Teacher	45%	67%
Clergy	44%	63%

92% of Canadians believe homosexuals should have equal rights in job opportunities; 61% say gay couples should have access to the same benefits as heterosexual couples.

— Gallup Polls, 2001

ENVIRONMENTAL ISSUES

**Canadian Sewage Treatment Approaches –
Best and worst practices**

Good

- Whitehorse no longer discharges into Yukon River – all sewage gets secondary treatment and UV disinfection
- Calgary – waste system receives advanced tertiary treatment – highest level available
- Bear River, NS – first community in Canada to implement Solar Aquatics waste-water treatment

Bad

- over 90 municipalities still dump raw sewage into waterways
- Victoria, BC discharges its sewage – 45B litres/year untreated into Pacific
- Dawson, Yukon dumps about 1B litres of raw sewage per year into Yukon River
- more than 30B litres of raw sewage are discharged annually into St. John's Harbour

— *Environment Canada*, May/June 2002

Waste diversion

Percentage of waste being diverted from landfill:

■ Guelph	52%
■ Vancouver	50%
■ Edmonton	45%
■ Halifax	43%
■ Montreal	41%
■ London	33%
■ Halton Region	31%
■ Ottawa	31%
■ Durham Region	29%
■ Peel Region	28%
■ Toronto	27%
■ York Region	26%
■ Hamilton	16%

Waste disposal in Canada

Kilograms per capita:

■ CANADA	750
■ Quebec	940
■ Alberta	910
■ Manitoba	819
■ Saskatchewan	811
■ Nfld.& Labrador	760
■ **Ontario**	**650**
■ British Columbia	640
■ New Brunswick	630
■ Nova Scotia	460
■ PEI	N/A
■ Yukon & NWT	N/A

(Statistics Canada)

International recycling

Percentage of household waste recycled:

■ Austria	50%
■ Germany	46%
■ Netherlands	43%
■ **Canada**	**42%**
■ Denmark	29%
■ Sweden	29%
■ US	28%
■ UK	11%
■ Ireland	9%
■ France	7%
■ Italy	3%
■ Spain	3%

(Institute of Wastes Management)

(CP/Brockville Recorder and Times/Darcy Cheek)

Right: An Ontario Provincial Police cruiser escorts a convoy of tractors, trucks and trailers loaded with hay as they enter the city of Brockville, Ontario, 23 July 2002. The hay relief effort for drought-stricken Prairie farmers attracted widespread attention in eastern Ontario – bales of all sizes and shapes were brought to the CN railyards in Brockville for shipment west.

Climate change effects like drought or mild winters have significant downstream economic impacts – particularly on natural resource industries and agriculture
- sparse 2001 rainfall caused Prairie drought – $5B in crop failures
- Southern Alberta's 2001 drought cycle reduced cattle herds by close to 5%
- Mountain Pine Beetle epidemic now accounts for 98% of the allowable annual cut in BC

— Climate Change Trends in Canada, *Environment Canada 2001-02*

(Thomas Boldt)

Grasshoppers plague province

Saskatchewan farms hit by worst drought in 133 years are unable to sustain livestock.

Scott Hartley, an insect specialist with the province of Saskatchewan says that "Grasshoppers are one of the most serious pests historically in Saskatchewan." This year, the hardest-hit areas are in the bone-dry, west-central part of the province. Some fields have been damaged so badly by drought and grasshoppers that farmers have been forced to cut their losses and file for preharvest insurance claims.

The worst drought in the West in 133 years has ruined cattle breeders' forage crops, leaving nothing to feed their livestock. Any crops left standing are being ravaged by the grasshoppers.

—Adapted from Allison Dunfield, Kim Lunman, *The Globe and Mail,* 24 July 2002

WORKPLACE HEALTH AND SAFETY

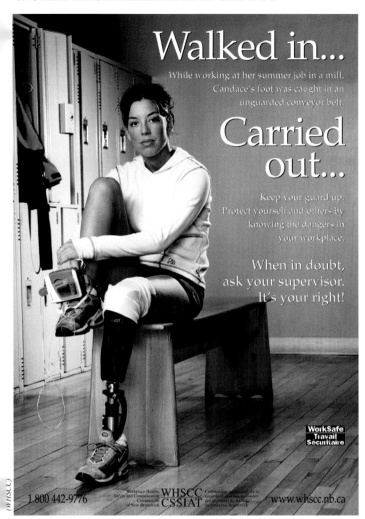

Walked in...

While working at her summer job in a mill, Candace's foot was caught in an unguarded conveyor belt.

Carried out...

Keep your guard up. Protect yourself and others by knowing the dangers in your workplace.

When in doubt, ask your supervisor. It's your right!

WorkSafe
Travail
Securitaire

1 800 442-9776

WHSCC
CSSIAT

Workplace Health, Safety and Compensation Commission of New Brunswick

Commission de la santé, de la sécurité et de l'indemnisation des accidents au travail du Nouveau-Brunswick

www.whscc.nb.ca

(WHSCC)

All provinces now have a special advocate or education program for young workers.

Work-related Deaths in B.C. (2001)

— Workers Compensation Board of B.C.

35% work-related disease (58 Workers)

65% single-incident (110 Workers)

FOOD & BEVERAGE SERVERS: HAZARDS

Biological & Chemical:
• bacteria [salmonella, E.coli] can spread from lack of hand washing
• possible contact with bleaches, cleaners, soaps and detergents.
• possible exposure to pesticides
• poor air quality and second-hand smoke.

Ergonomic & Physical:
• walking and standing for hours at a time; poor footwear;
• repetitive strain injuries (RSIs)
• improper lifting and carrying techniques may cause back strain.
• high noise levels from equipment, sound systems or patrons;
• good layout of dining room is important in preventing accidents;
• scalds and burns from hot food, hot liquids and hot equipment;
• electric shock or burns from stoves, ovens and faulty microwave ovens;

Safety:
• slips and falls on cluttered, or wet floors and stairs;
• injury to limbs from trapped hands, hair, baggy clothing or jewellery
• cuts from knives, chipped glassware and dishware;
• faulty electrical tools, appliances, wires, equipment;

Psychosocial:
• high stress/pressure from fast paced work and need to perform efficiently;
• shift work;
• uncertain income due to dependence on gratuities;
• dealing with irate or difficult customers;
• coping with patrons who leave without paying.

— Adapted from *Canadian Centre for Occupational Health and Safety*, 2002

THE JOB-CREATION REBOUND

Job creation in the first half of the year, 1977 to 2002

[Bar chart with y-axis from -400 to 400 and x-axis years 1977, 79, 81, 83, 85, 87, 89, 91, 93, 95, 97, 99, 2001]

Jobs for life. Union must be kidding

...How wonderful it would be if city ratepayers enjoyed the same protection as city workers. Imagine a guarantee that our property taxes will remain stable for at least 30 years. Or the assurance that service levels won't change for the next three decades.

City councillors hold their jobs for only three years before facing the voters. Nobody else enjoys guaranteed employment for life. Why should members of our city unions?

— Guy Giorno, *The Toronto Star*

What's wrong with wanting job security?

In fact, jobs for life is a distortion. The municipal workers are trying to hold onto the right to some job security after 10 years of service.

Of course, that sort of security is rare these days. But should we necessarily give in to the corporate vision of a world where workers are gradually stripped of all the protections they won in hard-fought battles over the last century?

...Of course, there has never been any evidence to back up that private sector-is-better assertion. Privatization generally just adds another layer – the private contractor – needing to be paid. So someone's got to be squeezed somewhere.

The squeeze hits the worker, who is replaced with a cheaper non-union worker. The savings allows the contractor to make a profit.

— Linda McQuaig, *The Toronto Star*

Over the past decade (1990-2000), union membership is down 100 000. For the first time since the 1960s, the overall percentage of unionized workers in the workforce in Canada has fallen below 30%.

— John Peters, "Labour at the Crossroads," *The Toronto Star*, 30 August 2002

Index

LEGEND:

AGO – Art Gallery of Ontario
BC – British Columbia Archives
CP – Canadian Press
CSTM – Canada Science and
   Technology Museum
CTA – City of Toronto Archives
CWM – Canadian War Museum
EA – City of Edmonton Archives
Glenbow – The Glenbow Archives
NAC – National Archives of Canada
NFB – National Film Board of Canada
SFU – Simon Fraser University
WAHC – Workers Arts and Heritage
   Museum